POUR: The Self-Nourishment Blueprint

By Tamar Jackson and Samuel Bradshaw

DEDICATION

From Tamar for Nova, Linkon, Syncere, Jaidyn, Jayda and Brandy

From Sam for Gordazo, Madeline, and Alana

by Tamar Jackson and Samuel Bradshaw

Published by Tamar Jackson and Samuel Bradshaw

Printed in the United States of America

First Edition, 2024

Table of Contents:

Chapter 1
Introduction to POUR

Tamar and I created POUR and this self-nourishment guidebook because we needed a way to care for ourselves in a post-pandemic world. We were exhausted, burned out, and not paying enough attention to what we were consuming physically, mentally, and emotionally. We weren't mindful of where we placed our energy, which left us drained and unable to recharge. Through deep conversations, one-on-one sessions, and the guidance of mentors, we developed a method that helped us recalibrate. It allowed us to recognize where our energy was going, better understand our environments, focus on our strengths and passions, and rebuild relationships with greater intention.

Our hope is that this guidebook helps you reclaim your energy, examine the influences shaping your life, harness your unique strengths, and cultivate healthier, more intentional relationships with yourself and the world around you. As people, we naturally form connections, investing our time, energy, and emotions into relationships. But not all relationships are equal, so it's essential to be mindful of where we direct our efforts both in giving and receiving.

"Pouring into others" means offering your time, energy, or resources to support those around you whether through emotional encouragement, financial assistance, or simply being a present and active listener. While this generosity can be deeply fulfilling, maintaining a balance is crucial to prevent burnout. When you POUR into others, you're sharing a part of yourself, and without intentional boundaries, you risk depleting your own reserves.

A fundamental principle of POUR is reciprocity. Building relationships with people who recognize and return your efforts leads to mutual growth and fulfillment. This doesn't mean every interaction should be transactional, but it does require setting boundaries to avoid the exhaustion of one-sided relationships.

Not everyone can or will give back in the same way, and that's okay. Instead of clinging to unfulfilling relationships, focus on those who genuinely support and uplift you in return. In short, "Pour into others who pour into you" serves as a reminder to invest your energy in relationships that foster mutual support. This mindset not only safeguards your well-being but also promotes personal growth. By prioritizing balanced, reciprocal connections, you cultivate a strong support system that empowers you and those around you to thrive, leading to a more fulfilling and successful life.

What is POUR?

POUR is a concept Tamar and I develop to reclaim our energy, our lives, our time and, most importantly, our peace. We use POUR to deepen our understanding of ourselves, practice meaningful self-care, pursue personal growth, and build or rebuild relationships with greater intention. The acronym POUR stands for four foundational principles:

Protecting your energy, observing your circle, unlocking your gifts and talents, and reigniting your purpose.

- **Tenet 1: Protecting Your Energy**

  The first tenet of POUR is Protecting Your Energy. This means recognizing the balance between caring for yourself and managing external commitments and taking intentional steps to safeguard your emotional and mental well-being.

  When you prioritize your energy, you prevent burnout and create a strong foundation for healthy, reciprocal relationships. Protecting your energy isn't selfish it's essential for showing up as your best self, both for you and for those you care about.

- **Tenet 2: Observing Your Circle**

  Observing Your Circle is about becoming aware of the relationships, habits, emotions, and behaviors that shape your daily life. This tenet invites you to evaluate and intentionally curate your social circle, making sure it aligns with your values and supports your goals.

  When you choose connections that nurture your growth, you create space for meaningful, fulfilling interactions built on mutual respect and understanding. By observing your circle, you empower yourself to surround your life with people and environments that reflect who you are and who you are becoming.

- **Tenet 3: Unlocking Your Gifts and Talents**

  Unlocking Your Gifts means recognizing and embracing your unique strengths and talents. When you bring your authentic self to your relationships, you naturally add value and create deeper connections. This principle emphasizes that understanding your truest self not only enhances the quality of your relationships but also lays the foundation for meaningful reciprocity.

- **Tenet 4: Reigniting Your Purpose**

Your purpose is never truly lost it only needs to be rediscovered and reignited. Over time, doubt, distractions, and societal pressures can dull your passion, leaving you feeling disconnected from what genuinely fulfills you. But purpose is not a destination; it's a lifelong journey of self-awareness and intentional action. By clearing mental clutter, embracing your unique gifts, and aligning your daily choices and relationships with your core values, you create space for purpose to thrive. This principle lays the foundation for reconnecting with what drives you, ensuring you move forward with clarity, fulfillment, and lasting impact.

What to Expect in This Book

As you work through this book, you'll explore each tenet of POUR Protect, Observe, Unlock, and Reignite and discover a clear framework for personal growth and deeper relationships. You'll read real-life examples of how POUR works, gain insights into building healthy connections with a focus on observation and reciprocity, and reflect on your strengths and areas for growth through practical exercises. You'll also learn actionable tips for managing your energy through self-care and setting boundaries. By embracing POUR, you create a path to a more fulfilling life and stronger, more authentic relationships.

What You Need to Be Prepared For

Early in this book, we focus on building self-awareness and setting meaningful goals. Through reflective journaling, you'll explore who you are your values, environment, and the boundaries you need to feel safe, protected, and nurtured.

Be open and honest with yourself as you dive into these core areas:

- **Self-Reflection:** Prepare to look inward, uncover your strengths, and recognize opportunities for growth. Assessing Relationships: Evaluate your social circles with fresh eyes, ensuring your connections align with your values and support your goals.
- **Embracing Change:** Resetting your life's table may require courageous shifts redefining priorities, setting healthier boundaries, or releasing relationships that no longer serve you.
- **Commitment to Reciprocity:** Understand the power of mutual support in relationships and be willing to invest in connections that give as much as they take.
- **Practical Strategies:** You'll gain actionable tools rooted in the POUR principles, designed to help you create a positive, fulfilling, and sustainable environment.
- **How to Use This Book:** Learn, Document, Act, Grow

Think of this book as more than just words on a page it's a personal growth toolkit, a guide designed to help you reset, realign, and reignite your sense of purpose. True transformation doesn't happen simply by reading; it requires engagement, reflection, and action. This book invites you to move beyond passive learning and actively participate in your own evolution.

Each chapter is intentionally crafted to challenge old patterns, deepen your self-awareness, and cultivate meaningful relationships. As you explore the concepts and exercises, approach them with curiosity and purpose. Your journey is unique, and this book is here to support you as you shape a life that reflects your values, aspirations, and gifts. Throughout this process, you'll discover what nurtures your growth and what holds you back. Transformation is not an instant shift it's a journey of small, intentional steps. With every exercise and reflection, you are building a stronger, more purpose-driven version of yourself.

- **Start with an Open Mind:** Be open to new ideas and self-discovery this mindset will help you absorb and apply the concepts in this book.
- **Understand the POUR Framework:** Learn each component of POUR Protect, Observe, Unlock, reignite and see how they

work together to support personal growth and strengthen relationships.

- **Engage in Self-Reflection:** Actively participate in the self-reflection exercises to uncover insights about your strengths, challenges, and opportunities for growth.
- **Apply Concepts to Your Life:** Connect the POUR principles to your real-life experiences. Use them to deepen relationships, advance your career, and cultivate personal fulfillment.
- **Set Personal Goals:** Define clear, achievable goals rooted in the POUR principles. These may include setting healthy boundaries, developing your strengths, or fostering reciprocal relationships.
- **Track Your Progress:** Regularly reflect on your journey. Notice the changes taking place, adjust your goals as needed, and embrace challenges as opportunities to grow.
- **Integrate Learnings into Daily Life:** Use the POUR principles as a guide for daily decisions, relationships, and how you show up in the world.
- **Celebrate Achievements:** Acknowledge and celebrate your successes along the way every step forward is meaningful progress.

Finding Your Center

This journey is about connecting with your core values and strengthening your sense of self in a world that often feels uncertain. It's about learning how to protect your energy while fully participating in life. You'll discover when to set boundaries, embrace new experiences, and navigate relationships all while prioritizing your well-being.

Personal growth is a process that takes time, so be patient and compassionate with yourself as you move through the chapters, exercises, and journal prompts. Treat yourself with kindness as you engage in this transformative work. Welcome to The Self-Nourishment Blueprint. We are honored to walk this journey with you

.

Chapter 2
Resetting the Table

In this chapter, we explore how your experiences, relationships, and emotions come together like a well-set table, each piece telling its own story. Picture this table as a symbol of your life, adorned with memories that have shaped who you are. Over time, though, this table may have become crowded, weighed down by unresolved emotions, hidden pain, and unspoken fears.

Resetting your table isn't just about rearranging what's there, it's about recognizing what feels cluttered, clearing away the past, and making room for the next chapters of your life.

Resetting your table takes care and intention. It's more than shifting things around; it's about creating space for growth. This means allowing yourself to quiet your mind, let go of what no longer serves you, and prepare for what's to come. Understanding yourself can be challenging even uncomfortable, but offering yourself patience and compassion is essential to growth. You deserve to create peace within your mind. To begin resetting your table, you must uncover the hidden pains you carry the silent struggles you may not have fully faced yet, like unresolved trauma, grief, or fears of abandonment. Confronting these pains is an act of courage, much like polishing a set of tarnished silverware. It takes time and effort, but by acknowledging these wounds, you open the door to healing and new possibilities.

Next, you need to address the fears that have settled into your life like unwanted guests. Whether it's fear of the unknown, self-doubt, or holding on to past identities, these fears can quietly take over and overshadow the life you want to live. Resetting your table begins by acknowledging these fears, understanding where they come from, and committing to work through them.

Ask yourself the tough questions — Why am I afraid? Have I been hurt before? Am I holding back because of low self-esteem? Facing these questions is the first step toward healing. Understanding your fears gives you the power to overcome them.

Resetting your table is about reclaiming control over your life and future. It's a bold declaration that you have the power to shape your own story. This means intentionally arranging your life in a way that reflects who you are today and who you are becoming. By facing your hidden pains and fears, you lay a strong foundation for personal growth and self-discovery. This is an act of self-love a commitment to living a life that honors your truth.

As you move forward, let this idea of resetting the table guide you. Uncover what has been hidden, face what has been feared, and embrace this journey of reclaiming your life. This is your path to a more authentic, resilient, and fulfilling life one that is fully your own.

Unveiling the Hidden: Embracing Growth by Facing Secret Pains

Freeing yourself from hidden pains begins with recognizing they are there. These pains often lie buried deep beneath layers of distraction, routine, and self-protection, yet they quietly shape how you see yourself, your relationships, and the world around you. Confronting them isn't about dwelling on the past it's about acknowledging the unspoken wounds that influence your choices, behaviors, and emotional well-being. This is not an act of weakness but one of profound courage. By facing what has been hidden, you open the door to healing, growth, and a life that reflects your truest self.

What Are Hidden Pains?

Hidden pains are the silent burdens we carry unresolved emotions, unspoken disappointments, past rejections, and lingering self-doubt we may not even realize are affecting us. These hidden wounds often stem from childhood experiences, broken relationships, societal expectations, or moments when we felt unseen, unheard, or unworthy.

Sometimes, these pains disguise themselves as fear, insecurity, or patterns of avoidance. Other times, they show up as perfectionism, people-pleasing, or an inability to fully trust or embrace joy. Society often urges us to "stay positive" or "just move on," but true personal growth isn't about suppressing pain it's about understanding it. When we ignore or bury our deeper struggles, they don't disappear; instead, they manifest in our choices, relationships, and emotional patterns.

Hidden pains shape how we love, how we set boundaries, how we pursue our goals, and how we see our worth. Until we bring them into the light and acknowledge them, they continue to shape us in ways we may not even realize.

Why Understanding Your Hidden Pains Matters

Recognizing these pains is not about fixing them overnight, nor is it about assigning blame. It is about allowing yourself to be honest and vulnerable with the parts of yourself that need healing. By taking the time to acknowledge these wounds, you create space for deeper self-awareness, acceptance, and transformation.

Hidden pains affect your relationships. When past wounds remain unaddressed, they can perpetuate patterns of distrust, emotional detachment, or fear of vulnerability. Recognizing these patterns helps you break free from cycles that no longer serve your growth. They influence your self-worth. Negative experiences or internalized beliefs from your past can manifest as self-doubt or hesitation, preventing you from pursuing what you genuinely desire. Understanding the origin of these beliefs empowers you to rewrite your narrative.

They shape your choices. Whether in your career, personal life, or daily habits, unexamined pain may cause you to settle for less, avoid risks, or remain trapped in comfortable but unfulfilling situations. Acknowledging these influences restores your agency in decision-making.

Healing does not erase the past it allows you to make peace with it. It involves seeing yourself clearly, free of judgment, and recognizing that you are deserving of the freedom brought about by self-awareness. By confronting what has been hidden, you reclaim your power and step confidently into who you are meant to become.

A Call to Explore and Release

This section is an invitation to explore the hidden pains you carry, not as something to fear, but as something to understand. Acknowledging them doesn't make you weak; in fact, it makes you stronger. It allows you to release the weight of past hurts and replace them with self-compassion, resilience, and clarity. Growth is not just about positivity it's about honesty. It is about meeting yourself where you are, with all your experiences, and choosing to move forward with a greater sense of awareness and self-love. The journey to healing starts with a single step: acknowledgment. What you have hidden no longer has to define you. You are in control of your story.

By doing this work, you are resetting the table not just clearing the surface but addressing what has been underneath it all along. And that is where real transformation begins.

Types of Hidden Pains

Hidden pains are deeply personal, often taking different forms depending on your individual life experiences:

Unresolved Trauma: Emotional wounds from past experiences can negatively shape your self-perception, relationships, and overall well-being.

Guilt or Shame: Lingering guilt or shame over past mistakes can erode self-esteem and impair your ability to connect with others.

Unexpressed Grief: Grief that remains unprocessed can manifest as hidden pain, negatively impacting emotional health.

Insecurity and Self-Doubt: Persistent feelings of insecurity and doubt can undermine confidence, limiting personal and professional growth.

Fear of Rejection or Abandonment: Past experiences of rejection or abandonment can cause relationship difficulties, triggering self-sabotage or anxiety about forming new connections.

Identity Crisis: Uncertainty regarding aspects of your identity such as gender, sexuality, or culture can create hidden pain and hinder self-acceptance.

Perfectionism: An obsessive drive for perfection, typically rooted in a fear of failure, can cause burnout, anxiety, and chronic dissatisfaction.

Betrayal Trauma: Emotional wounds caused by betrayal can severely damage trust, complicating future relationships.

Chronic Self-Criticism: Ongoing self-criticism erodes confidence, creating a persistent negative self-image.

Unfulfilled Dreams: Unaddressed or suppressed desires can diminish life satisfaction; acknowledging them is essential for achieving a meaningful life.

These examples illustrate the complexity of hidden pain, though they don't encompass every struggle. Exploring and addressing these internal challenges is a courageous step toward healing, growth, and a more authentic life.

Reflective Engagement Prompt

As you begin this journey of self-discovery, take a moment to reflect on your inner world. The following prompts are designed to help you explore the hidden pains you may carry. Use them as gentle guides to journal your thoughts and let the process unfold naturally. You may choose one or more prompts that resonate with you, but consider spending time with each one.

Remember, the goal isn't to "complete" this exercise it's to open the door to greater self-awareness and prepare yourself for what lies ahead.

Reflection Prompts for Exploring Hidden Pain

Recognition and Awareness: Reflect on moments when you've become aware of hidden pains in your life. What specific experiences or emotions stand out? Impact on Decision-Making: Consider how these hidden pains may have influenced your decisions, relationships, and overall well-being. What patterns or recurring themes do you notice in your life?

Facing Resistance: Explore areas where you may have resisted acknowledging or confronting these pains. What emotions arise when you think about facing them directly?

Emotional Weight: Reflect on the emotional burden of unaddressed pain. How does carrying these weights affect your daily life, relationships, and sense of self?

Coping Mechanisms: Examine the ways you've learned to cope with these hidden pains. Have these strategies been helpful, or do they sometimes create additional struggles?

What Could Be Better: Imagine how your life might improve if you acknowledged and began to work through these pains. What would healing look and feel like for you?

Find a quiet space, let your thoughts flow freely, and gently explore the depths of your inner world. This reflective process is an essential step toward understanding and eventually releasing the hidden pains that may be woven into your life. Remember, this is a journey of self-compassion and growth and it's only the beginning.

Navigating Fears in Personal Growth: A Journey to Self-Discovery

As you continue your journey of personal growth, it's essential to recognize the fears that may be holding you back. These fears often act as unseen barriers to change, quietly shaping how you navigate the path of self-discovery. Each fear presents its own unique challenge, influencing your transformation in subtle but significant ways.

Let's explore some of the most common fears that often accompany personal growth.

- **Fear of the Unknown:** When we step into new areas of personal growth, fear of the unknown often surfaces. This fear breeds doubts about what lies ahead, causing us to question whether it's worth taking the risk to explore unfamiliar territory.
- **Comfort Zone Reluctance:** Our comfort zone a space of familiarity and routine may feel safe, but it can also be limiting. The fear of leaving this zone often stems from not wanting to disrupt the stability we've built.

- **Self-Doubt and Low Self-Esteem:** Internal fears, such as self-doubt and low self-esteem, can lead us to question our ability to grow. Overcoming these fears means challenging negative beliefs about our worth and potential.
- **Fear of Failure:** The fear of failure looms large, making us hesitant to take risks. Often, we tie our self-worth to success, which makes the journey of personal growth feel overwhelming.
- **Resistance to Vulnerability:** Growth requires vulnerability being open, authentic, and willing to confront discomfort. Yet, fear of judgment or rejection can make us resist this openness, slowing our transformation.
- **Attachment to Past Identities:** As we grow, our old identities may no longer fit. Fear arises when we cling to these outdated versions of ourselves, making it harder to embrace who we are becoming.
- **Lack of Self-Awareness:** Sometimes, we fear looking inward either because we're avoiding what we might find or because we underestimate the power of self-awareness. This fear can keep us disconnected from ourselves and hinder true growth.
- **External Expectations:** Societal norms and family pressures can create fear around stepping off the expected path. Overcoming this fear requires finding balance honoring what

others hope for us while staying true to what we genuinely want.

By recognizing and addressing these fears, you can pave the way for a more authentic, resilient, and fulfilling journey of self-discovery.

- **Reflective Exploration:** Uncovering Your Personal Fears

  Take time to explore the subtle fears that may be quietly holding you back from personal growth. Reflect on the prompts below to deepen your understanding of these fears because recognizing them is the first step toward unlocking a more authentic and fulfilling version of yourself.

1. Fear of the Unknown

Consider an area of your life where fear of the unknown is keeping you stuck. What uncertainties are you avoiding, and how might facing them help you grow?

2. Comfort Zone Reluctance

Think about the parts of your life where you've grown comfortable. What routines or habits have become your safe haven? How could stepping beyond these comfort zones open new doors for growth?

3. Self-Doubt and Low Self-Esteem

Reflect on moments when self-doubt has shaped your decisions. Where do you struggle with low self-esteem, and how might shifting these beliefs support your growth?

4. Fear of Failure

Identify a goal or dream you've hesitated to pursue because of a fear of failing. What small steps can you take to redefine success separating it from perfection and embrace the lessons that setbacks can offer?

5. Resistance to Vulnerability

Think about times when you've avoided being vulnerable. How has this shaped your relationships and personal growth? How might embracing vulnerability lead to deeper connections and greater self-discovery?

6. Attachment to Past Identities

Consider aspects of your past identity that you still hold onto. How could letting go of these old selves help you become who you're meant to be? What new parts of your identity are you ready to embrace?

7. Lack of Self-Awareness

Reflect on areas of your life where self-awareness may be missing. What emotions or patterns are you overlooking? How could greater self-understanding lead to a more purposeful life?

8. External Expectations

Examine the expectations placed on you by society, family, or friends. Which of these align with your true desires, and which ones hold you back? How can you navigate these pressures while staying true to yourself?

By exploring your fears across different areas of life people, places, habits, and emotions you can uncover where you are on your journey and where you want to go. Even when change feels intimidating, acknowledging and understanding your fears is the first step toward becoming your most authentic self.

Exercise: "Pathway to Where You're Going"

This exercise aims to help you reflect on your current situation and envision the path Once upon a time, in a place called [Current Situation], I realize that I must leave behind [Negative Habits, Behaviors, or Mindsets] that hold me back. It becomes clear that if I want to reach [Desired Destination], I need to let go of those limiting patterns.

Letting go of [Negative Habit, Behavior, or Mindset] is not easy, but I know it is essential for my growth. As I take my first steps away from it, I feel a mix of [Emotion], [Emotion], and [Emotion]. The path ahead feels [Adjective], and I am uncertain about what lies beyond.

Yet, as I walk away from [Negative Habit, Behavior, or Mindset], I begin to notice [Positive Change or Insight]. It's as though a weight has lifted from my shoulders, and suddenly I can see [New

Perspective or Opportunity] on the horizon. I realize that reaching [Desired Destination] requires surrounding myself with [Positive Influence] and focusing on [Personal Value or Goal].

With each step forward, I feel more connected to my true self. I understand that by leaving [Negative Habit, Behavior, or Mindset] behind, I am creating space for [Positive Change or Habit] to thrive. My energy shifts, and a sense of [New Emotion] fills me as I embrace this journey of self-discovery.

Along the way, as I move toward [Desired Destination], I face challenges and encounter opportunities I never imagined. Each one teaches me profound lessons about [Personal Growth or Learning]. I discover that by releasing what no longer serves me, I open the door for [Positive Outcome] to enter my life.

And so, as I look ahead to [Desired Destination], I feel grateful for the courage it took to let go of [Negative Habits, Behaviors, or Mindsets]. I am eager to continue nurturing [Positive Change or Habit], cultivating [Personal Value or Goal], and moving toward a future filled with [Desired Outcome] and [Positive Emotion].

Discussion and Reflection

After finishing the exercise, take time to reflect on how letting go of certain things can help you grow both personally and professionally.

This exercise is designed to help you reset your priorities and begin making positive, meaningful changes in your life.

Reflecting on Letting Go of Negativity:

What negative habit or mindset did you choose to leave behind?

Reflect on the specific mindset or behavior that no longer serves you. What have you been holding onto that keeps you from moving forward? Naming it is the first step toward real change. How did it feel to realize that letting go was necessary for your growth?

Acknowledging that something needs to change can be difficult. What emotions surfaced when you recognized that this habit or mindset was holding you back? How did that realization shift your perspective on growth and progress?

Emotional Journey

When you first began moving away from the negative habit or mindset, what emotions did you experience?

Describe the mix of feelings fear, doubt, relief, or hope that showed up in those early moments. Let yourself be honest about how hard or freeing it was to take that first step.

How did those emotions evolve as you continued on your path?

Growth is rarely a straight line. As you moved forward, did you notice moments of strength and clarity? Did fear give way to confidence? Reflect on how your emotional landscape shifted with each step away from negativity.

Positive Changes and New Insights

What positive changes or insights emerged as you distanced yourself from negativity? Describe the internal and external shifts you noticed. Were you thinking more clearly? Did you gain new opportunities or relationships? What did you learn about yourself in the process? How did letting go of unproductive behaviors create space for new perspectives or opportunities?

Sometimes, release is what makes room for growth. Reflect on the specific ways that freeing yourself from old patterns allowed new insights, opportunities, or relationships to emerge.

Surrounding Yourself with Positivity

This journey highlights the importance of being around positive influences. How will you intentionally bring positivity into your life?

Who do you need to connect with? What environments or communities will support your growth? Consider what practical steps you can take to surround yourself with uplifting people and influences.

What impact do you believe these positive influences will have on your journey toward your goals?

Think about how being around people who inspire and support you will impact your mindset, decisions, and outcomes. Why is this essential for your continued growth?

Connection to Personal Values and Goals

What personal value or goal are you focusing on? Why is it important to your journey?

Identify a value or goal that feels central to the person you are becoming. Why does this matter to you? How does it align with the life you want to create?

How do you plan to prioritize and nurture this value or goal in your daily life?

Think about real-life actions small or big that will help you honor this value or goal. How will you keep it front and center as you move forward?

Challenges and Opportunities

What challenges have you faced as you let go of what no longer serves you? What did you learn from these experiences?

Share a specific challenge that tested you. What lessons did you draw from overcoming it? How did facing that obstacle make you stronger?

How did releasing old patterns create room for positive outcomes in your life? Reflect on what entered your life once you made space. Did you gain peace, confidence, or new opportunities? What has been the reward for your courage to let go?

Gratitude and Excitement for the Future

Why are you grateful for having the courage to leave behind the negative habit or mindset?

Express gratitude for the growth you've experienced. How has your life changed for the better?

What excites you most as you continue embracing positive change and working toward your goals?

Look ahead. What are you hopeful for? What dreams or opportunities are now within reach because of your transformation?

Applying Insights to Real Life

How will you apply the insights from this exercise to your everyday life?

Consider how these lessons will influence your choices, relationships, and mindset going forward.

Are there specific actions you're now committed to taking to help you reach your goals? Name a few actionable steps even small ones that you are ready to implement starting now.

Looking Ahead

How has this exercise helped you reset your priorities and create positive change?

Take a moment to reflect on how your focus has shifted. What matters most now, and how will you keep that in view?

What steps will you take next to keep moving toward your desired destination?

Be intentional. What are the next right steps for you to stay on the path of growth, healing, and success?

The Power of Knowing Your Core Values

Your core values serve as an internal compass, shaping your mindset, guiding your behavior, and influencing your decisions. They help you identify what truly matters so you can navigate life with clarity, confidence, and intention.

When you make choices that align with your values, you experience a deeper sense of fulfillment, purpose, and emotional stability. But when your actions conflict with your values, you may feel uneasy, frustrated, or disconnected from yourself as if something essential is out of place. Embracing your core values goes beyond personal growth; it lays the foundation for a life that reflects your authentic self. Here's why your values matter:

They provide clarity and direction. Your values help you make decisions with confidence, ensuring that you are moving in a direction that is meaningful and fulfilling.

They shape your mindset. By focusing on what truly matters, you develop a mindset that is aligned with positivity, purpose, and resilience.

They strengthen your relationships. When you understand your own values, you can build deeper, more authentic connections with others who share or respect them.

They help you set boundaries. Knowing your values makes it easier to recognize what aligns with your well-being and what drains your energy, allowing you to protect your emotional and mental space.

They build self-trust. When your choices reflect your values, you reinforce trust in yourself, allowing you to navigate life with confidence and authenticity.

By identifying and embracing your core values, you create the foundation for lasting transformation. They serve as the blueprint for resetting the table, ensuring that the life you build is one that reflects your true essence.

Authenticity: Living in Alignment with Your Values

One of the greatest benefits of understanding your core values is that it empowers you to live authentically to make decisions and take actions that genuinely reflect who you are. Authenticity isn't about being perfect; it's about being real. It's about making choices that feel right in your soul, even when they go against the expectations of others.

When your values and actions are aligned, you experience a profound sense of purpose and clarity. You stop making decisions out of obligation and start making them with intention. You no longer seek validation from external sources because you are grounded in the truth of who you are. Authenticity becomes a way of life, not just an ideal.

Living in alignment with your values also transforms how you connect with others. It allows you to build relationships based on mutual respect and shared principles, rather than convenience or habit. It equips you to navigate challenges with integrity and resilience, knowing your actions are rooted in what truly matters.

Yet, embracing authenticity takes courage. It means being willing to step away from situations, habits, and even relationships that no longer reflect your values. It requires trusting yourself enough to choose what is right for you, even when it's hard. This is what resetting the table is all about clearing away what no longer serves you and intentionally rebuilding your life with what does.

Your Values as the Foundation for a New Mindset

Now that you understand the power of your values and how they shape your life, it's time to take action. The next step is to engage in a values definition exercise an intentional process to clarify and prioritize what truly matters to you. This isn't just a theoretical exercise; it's a practical, hands-on tool for self-discovery that helps you define the principles guiding your decisions, relationships, and aspirations.

Through this exercise, you will:

Identify your core values the non-negotiable principles that define who you are.

Reflect on why they matter and how they influence your choices and actions.

Assess whether your current mindset and lifestyle align with these values. Create a plan to realign your life, making intentional shifts to ensure you are living in alignment with what you truly believe. As you move forward, these core values will serve as the foundation for your decisions, your relationships, and your mindset. They will empower you to reset your table with clarity, purpose, and intention ensuring that the life you create is aligned, fulfilling, and unapologetically yours.

It's time to define your values. It's time to reset the table. It's time to live on purpose.

Exercise: "My Values Blueprint"

Create a visual representation of your core values. This could take the form of a mind map, a list, or any creative format that resonates with you.

Write a brief paragraph explaining why each value is significant to you.

Aligning Your Values

In this next step of your journey, we focus on the core values that guide your decisions, actions, and relationships. Staying true to these values is essential for creating a life that genuinely reflects who you are.

Exercise: "Core Values Alignment" Draw a table with columns representing key areas of your life (e.g., relationships, career, personal growth). (Leave space for this table on a blank page.)

Assess how well each area aligns with your core values. Use symbols, colors, or a rating system to indicate the level of alignment.

Write short notes on adjustments or intentional actions you can take to strengthen that alignment.

Discussion on Aligning Your Values

At the heart of every meaningful and fulfilling life are core values principles, qualities, and beliefs that define who you are and guide your decisions. Aligning your life with these values creates a solid foundation that sustains both your purpose and well-being. But in the fast pace of daily life, it's easy to lose sight of what truly matters. That's why it's essential to pause, reflect, and reconnect with those values.

Begin by identifying three core values that matter most to you. These might be qualities such as integrity, growth, connection, or creativity anything that deeply resonates with who you are at your core. Take a moment to reflect on why these values are meaningful and how they shape your decisions, relationships, and ambitions. Do you see these values actively present in your daily life, or have certain habits, obligations, or outside influences drawn you away from them? By focusing on these core values, you'll gain clarity and direction, allowing you to live more intentionally rather than following patterns dictated by external expectations.

Your values don't just shape your personal goals they define the quality of your relationships. The people you spend time with have a powerful impact on your energy, mindset, and overall fulfillment.

Reflect for a moment: Do your closest relationships align with and support your core values? Are there connections that feel out of sync, creating tension or draining your energy? Strengthening relationships that uphold your values and setting boundaries with those that don't is crucial for building a life that feels authentic and purposeful.

Values also act as a compass in decision-making. Consider a recent choice you made big or small and ask yourself whether it aligned with your values. When decisions are rooted in what matters most, they bring clarity and confidence. But when they go against your values, they often leave behind unease or regret. By regularly aligning your actions with your core beliefs, you'll become more empowered and intentional in shaping the life you truly want. Recognize that your values can evolve over time. Who you were five or ten years ago may not be who you are today, and that's perfectly natural. Life experiences continually shape and refine what you hold dear, and part of this journey is allowing yourself the flexibility to grow and reassess. Reflect on how your values may have shifted and consider what that means for your goals, relationships, and priorities moving forward.

As we wrap up this chapter, take a moment to envision the table you've set a space free of outdated obligations, misaligned relationships, and distractions that no longer serve you. Instead, your table is thoughtfully arranged, with your values at the center, guiding every decision and shaping the path ahead. This process of realignment goes beyond self-reflection; it's about intentionally creating a life that genuinely reflects who you are and what you stand for.

This values assessment lays the foundation for profound self-discovery and sets the stage for the journey ahead. In the coming chapters, we'll explore how to Protect, Observe, Unlock, and Reignite within the framework of your values, offering tools for transformative growth. For now, savor the clarity you've uncovered, celebrate the insights you've gained, and embrace the opportunities that lie ahead. The table is set; the journey continues.

Chapter 3
Protecting Your Energy

Life often feels chaotic, and in the rush of daily demands, we tend to overlook one of our most important resources: our energy. This finite reserve fuels our mental and physical well-being, making it vital to consider where and how we spend it. In this chapter, we'll examine practical ways to safeguard this resource, integrate self-care, pursue long-term goals, nurture relationships, and maintain inner peace. Since every day involves countless demands from family obligations to career challenges it's crucial that we invest our energy in ways that genuinely enrich our lives.

Why Protecting Energy Matters

Your energy is one of your most valuable resources it powers your actions, shapes your decisions, and sustains your overall well-being. But unlike time, which passes regardless of what we do, energy requires intentional management, protection, and replenishment. When you continuously give it away without deliberate recovery, you risk facing exhaustion, frustration, and burnout. Being mindful of where and how you invest your energy ensures you can focus it on what truly matters most.

Think of energy as a bank account. Every task, interaction, or commitment represents a withdrawal, while rest, self-care, and meaningful experiences serve as deposits. If you continue to withdraw without replenishing, your balance will eventually hit zero. Small, enjoyable activities such as a fun night out with friends or indulging in a favorite hobby can provide quick boosts. Yet, too many impulsive withdrawals like overcommitting, excessive socializing, or endless mindless scrolling can leave you drained, distracted, and unmotivated.

By carefully choosing how to spend your energy, you create space for lasting fulfillment rather than fleeting rewards. Skipping short-term indulgences allows you to stay focused on meaningful objectives, whether improving your health, advancing your career, or deepening your relationships. Protecting your energy gives you the best chance at sustainable success and ensures that you're not just busy, but genuinely fulfilled.

Setting Boundaries with Others

Setting boundaries is a vital part of protecting your energy. Boundaries act as invisible lines that define where your energy starts and ends, clarifying how much you're willing to give and ensuring you don't overextend yourself. Without them, it's all too easy to feel drained, resentful, or even burned out especially when others constantly seek your time, help, or emotional support.

It's important to remember that boundaries are not walls. They're not meant to shut people out. Instead, boundaries serve as guidelines, helping you protect your energy while remaining present and supportive in ways that work for you. Think of them as a proactive tool for managing relationships, whether they're with friends, family, or coworkers.

Consider a friend who frequently vents about their problems but never asks how you're doing. It's okay to kindly express that while you're happy to listen, you also need time to recharge. You might say, "I'm happy to support you, but I need time to recharge my energy, so I can't always be available." This gentle statement respects both your friend's need to share and your own need for personal space.

Setting boundaries may feel uncomfortable at first, especially if you're used to always being available for others. Some people might react negatively, but remember that boundaries are an expression of respect not just for yourself but for the relationship as a whole. Healthy boundaries create clearer expectations, allowing both parties to feel comfortable and understood.

Boundaries also enable us to offer our best to others without depleting ourselves. When you preserve your energy and say "yes" only when it aligns with your capacity, you can be fully present and engaged. For instance, limiting the time you spend on certain activities or setting clear expectations such as letting coworkers know you won't be checking emails after hours can make a significant difference. Ultimately, boundaries empower you to give from a place of abundance rather than obligation. By maintaining boundaries, you ensure that you can remain supportive and caring without feeling drained. It's a win-win for both you and the people in your life.

Understanding the Value of Your Energy

Your energy is a limited but powerful resource that affects every area of your life from relationships and career to personal well-being. By recognizing its value, you can make more deliberate decisions about where and how to direct it. Just like time or money, energy must be managed carefully. Constantly giving without taking time to recharge can lead to fatigue, frustration, and emotional burnout. Consider a moment when you've come home exhausted after a long day, only to snap at a loved one over something small. That reaction likely wasn't about them it was about you running on empty. When we're mentally and emotionally drained, even minor interactions can feel overwhelming. This is why understanding what depletes your energy versus what restores it is crucial. If you know certain tasks, environments, or individuals leave you feeling drained, you can plan ahead: take time to rest before a big event, build in time to recover afterward, or simply decline commitments that don't serve your well-being.

It's also important to notice when others are consistently overusing your energy. Healthy relationships are built on mutual respect and support, not one-sided emotional labor. If someone continually demands your time, attention, or emotional resources without giving anything in return, it might be time to set boundaries. Protecting your energy isn't selfish; it's essential for maintaining your emotional and mental health. By setting and upholding boundaries, you ensure your energy is valued and respected, giving you more freedom to invest it in the people and activities that truly fulfill and energize you.

Learning to Say "No": Reclaiming Your Energy and Priorities

Saying "no" is one of the most powerful ways to protect your energy, yet it's often one of the hardest. Many people struggle to turn down requests, commitments, or social invitations because they fear disappointing others, appearing selfish, or missing out. In reality, constantly saying "yes" to everyone and everything usually leads to exhaustion, resentment, and burnout. Every time you say "yes" to something that drains you, you are unintentionally saying "no" to something else often your well-being, peace of mind, or personal priorities. Learning to say "no" isn't about shutting people out or refusing to help; it's about choosing how to spend your time and energy wisely. By prioritizing your health and happiness, you can show up as a more present, supportive version of yourself for the people who matter most.

Think of "no" as a boundary-setting tool that helps you maintain balance and clarity. Without boundaries, your time and energy become scattered, making it difficult to stay aligned with your purpose. Saying "no" may feel uncomfortable at first, especially if you're used to accommodating others at your own expense. But, like any skill, the more you practice, the easier it becomes. Each time you set a boundary, you reaffirm your commitment to protecting your well-being and that is an act of self-care, not selfishness.

The Art of Saying "No" with Confidence and Compassion

Saying "no" effectively is both an art and a skill one that requires confidence, clarity, and compassion. It's natural to feel the urge to over-explain, apologize, or soften your refusal to avoid upsetting others. However, you don't need to offer lengthy justifications for prioritizing your own well-being. A simple, firm, and respectful "no" is often enough.

Mastering this skill involves finding a way to say "no" that respects both your boundaries and your relationships. If declining a request feels difficult, consider using a direct yet kind approach, such as:

"I appreciate you thinking of me, but I can't commit to that right now."

"I'm at my limit and need to focus on my priorities."

"I can't take this on at the moment, but I'd love to support you in another way." If you truly want to help but can't at the moment, you might offer an alternative: "I can't do it this week, but could we revisit it another time?"

"I don't have the capacity to handle the full task, but I'd be happy to help in a smaller way."

A well-placed "no" isn't a rejection of the person it's a reinforcement of your boundaries. The more you practice saying it confidently, the less stressful it becomes. Over time, protecting your energy allows you to be more intentional with your time, more present in your relationships, and more in control of your life. Saying "no" isn't about limitation it's about liberation. Respecting your own limits creates the space you need to focus on the opportunities, relationships, and experiences that truly support your well-being and personal growth.

Communicating Energy Needs: Honoring Yourself While Strengthening Relationships

Protecting your energy isn't just about knowing when to say "no." It's also about clearly communicating your needs to those around you. Often, people hesitate to share when they're feeling drained, worrying they'll come across as unreliable, distant, or uninterested. In reality, setting clear expectations around your energy levels strengthens relationships rather than weakens them. When you communicate honestly and confidently, you invite others to respect your boundaries while demonstrating the importance of self-care.

Picture this: you come home after a long, exhausting day at work and receive an invitation to go out with friends. On another day, you'd be thrilled to join, but right now, you're completely drained. Instead of pushing yourself to go, you can simply respond with a direct yet polite message: *"I had a rough day and really need to recharge tonight, so I'll have to skip. I hope you all have a great time!"* This small act of honesty and self-awareness not only protects your energy but also signals to others that your well-being is important. It alleviates unnecessary guilt because saying no to an invitation isn't the same as rejecting the people behind it. Instead, it's about understanding your own limits and making choices that support your overall health.

Effective energy communication isn't limited to social invitations. It applies to work, family, and any situation where you feel overextended. If a colleague asks for help but you're already at full capacity, you might respond with:

"I'd love to help, but I'm at full capacity right now. Can we check in later this week?"

Likewise, if a loved one needs emotional support but you're not in the right headspace to give it, you can express your limits without shutting them out:

"I really want to be here for you, but I'm feeling emotionally drained right now. Could we talk tomorrow when I can give you my full attention?"

Being honest about your energy levels allows you to maintain balance while fostering healthier, more understanding relationships. People who value you will appreciate your candor and respect your boundaries. At its core, expressing your energy needs is an act of self-respect and emotional intelligence. When you regularly communicate your need for rest, space, or time to recharge, you create a life where your energy is respected, your boundaries are clear, and your relationships become more authentic and supportive.

Empowerment: Taking Charge of Your Energy

Recognizing the value of your energy isn't just about self-awareness it's about reclaiming control over your life. Too often, we go through the day on autopilot, reacting to demands and obligations without considering how they affect our well-being. When you begin to see your energy as a limited, valuable resource, you shift from simply managing your life to actively shaping it with intention.

Managing your energy means making choices that truly serve you—not just what others expect of you. It's no longer about feeling obligated to meet every request or stretching yourself too thin. Instead, it's about deciding, with purpose, where your energy is best spent. For example, if you know you need downtime after a demanding day, you can set that boundary guilt-free. Rest isn't a luxury; it's a necessity. These small, intentional choices help lay the foundation for a more balanced, fulfilling life. Taking charge of your energy also shifts the way you make decisions. Instead of saying "yes" Out of habit or obligation, you might find yourself asking: Is this worth my time and effort? Does this align with my well-being and goals? By filtering your commitments through this perspective, you gain the confidence to say "no" when something doesn't serve you. This shift in mindset allows you to focus on what truly matters, ensuring your energy is directed toward growth, fulfillment, and the life you want to create.

As you embrace this approach, consider the impact of these choices. How has protecting your energy shaped your well-being, relationships, and daily life? What challenges have arisen along the way? Taking a step back to evaluate both the benefits and the obstacles of energy management helps you refine your strategy and move forward with clarity and confidence.

By valuing our energy, we take charge of our own path. We're not just passengers; we're the ones steering. This perspective fosters a strong sense of agency, reinforcing the idea that we deserve our time and care. In this way, energy management becomes both a form of self-respect and a foundation for a more fulfilling life. Reflecting on Your Energy: The Impact of Boundaries and Balance Taking charge of your energy isn't just about setting boundaries—it's about recognizing how those choices ripple across every area of your life. Protecting your energy doesn't only help in the moment; it fosters long-term benefits that shape your well-being, productivity, and relationships. Like any meaningful shift, it comes with challenges, but reflecting on both the positive outcomes and potential obstacles helps you refine your approach and maintain a healthy balance.

The Positive Impact of Energy Awareness

Improved Well-being: When you protect your energy, you often experience profound emotional and physical benefits. Think back to a time when saying "no" to something draining left you feeling lighter, happier, or more at peace. How has making your energy a priority helped reduce stress and improve your daily life?

Increased Productivity: By saying "no" to commitments and distractions that deplete you, you free up time and mental clarity for what truly matters. Have you noticed that managing your energy makes you more present and efficient? Consider how focusing your energy has helped you move closer to your personal and professional goals.

Stronger, Healthier Relationships: Clear boundaries foster respect and improve the quality of your relationships. Think about a time when you communicated your needs and felt genuinely heard. How has setting limits allowed you to build more fulfilling, supportive connections?

Greater Resilience: Protecting your energy—even in challenging situations—builds strength and confidence. Recall a moment when standing firm in your boundaries helped you navigate a difficult situation. How has asserting yourself made you more resilient under pressure or in the face of high expectations?

A Sense of Empowerment: Recognizing your control over where your energy goes can be transformative. Have you experienced a moment when prioritizing yourself led to greater self-trust and intentional decision-making? Consider how protecting your energy has allowed you to live more in alignment with your values.

The Challenges of Protecting Your Energy

Stronger, Healthier Relationships: Clear boundaries foster respect and improve the quality of your relationships. Think about a time when you communicated your needs and felt genuinely heard. How has setting limits allowed you to build more fulfilling, supportive connections?

Greater Resilience: Protecting your energy—even in challenging situations—builds strength and confidence. Recall a moment when standing firm in your boundaries helped you navigate a difficult situation. How has asserting yourself made you more resilient under pressure or in the face of high expectations?

A Sense of Empowerment: Recognizing your control over where your energy goes can be transformative. Have you experienced a moment when prioritizing yourself led to greater self-trust and intentional decision-making? Consider how protecting your energy has allowed you to live more in alignment with your values.

Finding Your Balance

There is no single formula for protecting your energy—it's a continuous practice of self-awareness, reflection, and adjustment. As you take control of your energy, revisit these questions regularly. Doing so will help you refine your approach, overcome obstacles, and maintain a balance that nurtures both your well-being and personal growth. Your energy is invaluable. Honoring it isn't just self-care—it's self-respect.

Protecting Your Energy: Strategies and Exercises

Navigating both the positive and negative aspects of energy protection requires practical tools and exercises that strengthen your ability to safeguard your energy. Below are actionable strategies to help you cultivate a balanced and sustainable approach to energy management.

Strategies

Set Boundaries Boundaries define where your energy is spent and prevent you from overextending yourself. Clearly establish what you are and aren't comfortable with, and communicate this assertively yet respectfully. Learning to say "no" without guilt is a crucial aspect of this practice. Setting boundaries honors your limits and preserves energy for what truly matters.

Identify Energy Drainers

Recognizing situations, environments, or individuals that consistently deplete your energy allows you to manage your exposure to these influences. Whether it means reducing time with certain people, setting clear expectations, or limiting involvement in draining activities, this strategy empowers you to make mindful choices about how you invest your energy.

Surround Yourself with Positive Influences

Prioritize relationships with people who uplift, support, and bring positivity into your life. These connections replenish rather than drain your energy, fostering a healthier emotional and mental balance. Focusing on interactions that nourish your well-being helps sustain your energy levels and prevent burnout.

Practice Intentional Self-Care Prioritizing self-care is essential for maintaining a balanced energy flow. This can include physical activities, mindfulness practices, or creative pursuits that bring you joy and relaxation. By making self-care a non-negotiable part of your routine, you actively replenish energy, enhance resilience, and reduce stress.

Manage Stress Managing stress through techniques like deep breathing, mindfulness, and physical activity helps regulate your energy. Identify healthy outlets for stress—whether through exercise, creative expression, or other personal activities—that allow you to release tension constructively. Proactively managing stress prevents energy depletion and enhances overall well-being.

Prioritize Meaningful Relationships

Invest in relationships that are reciprocal and enriching. Set boundaries with individuals who consistently take without giving, as one-sided connections can be emotionally draining. Nurturing positive, balanced relationships fosters a supportive environment and sustains your energy.

Protect Your Time with Intention

Guarding your time is essential to preserving energy. Prioritize commitments that align with your personal and professional goals, and be mindful of where you invest your efforts. Avoid overcommitting to tasks that drain you, and instead, focus on what brings you the most fulfillment and long-term benefit. Exercises Visualize a Protective Shield Imagine an invisible shield surrounding you, effortlessly deflecting negative energy while allowing positive energy to flow freely. This mental tool is especially useful in challenging situations, helping you remain grounded, focused, and unaffected by negativity.

Cord-Cutting Meditation

Close your eyes and visualize any draining energy connections as cords tethered to you. Now, imagine cutting these cords with a sharp, empowering force—releasing yourself from unwanted attachments. As you sever each cord, replace the empty space with revitalizing, positive energy. This technique is especially powerful for reinforcing boundaries after emotionally taxing interactions.

Mindful Breathing

Take a deep, purposeful breath. Inhale calm, positive energy. Exhale all tension and negativity. With each breath, feel yourself becoming more centered, present, and balanced. This simple yet transformative exercise can be practiced anytime to reset your focus and clear away unwanted emotions.

Create a Personal Energy Sanctuary Imagine a safe, tranquil space within your mind where you can retreat to recharge and restore your energy. Fill this space with comforting elements—soothing sounds, soft colors, familiar scents, or cherished memories. Let this mental refuge become a place you can return to whenever you feel overwhelmed or in need of peace.

Journaling

Reflect on the interactions, situations, and emotions that influence your energy. Journaling offers insight into the patterns that either drain or replenish you. By putting your thoughts to paper, you gain clarity and can develop personalized strategies to protect and sustain your energy.

Positive Affirmations

Speak affirmations that reinforce your worth, strength, and resilience. These powerful statements—such as "I am enough," "My energy is sacred," or "I choose to release what no longer serves me"—can uplift and remind you of your inner power. Positive affirmations are simple yet effective tools to keep you grounded and empowered.

Energetic Clearing Rituals

Engage in intentional rituals that help you release negative energy and invite calm. Practices like burning sage, working with crystals, or taking a cleansing salt bath can serve as symbolic resets. These actions promote mental clarity, emotional healing, and create space for positivity to flow back into your life.

Enhance Your Personal Energy Management

Regular reflection on personal energy management is essential for maintaining well-being and sustaining productivity. Use the following prompts to assess and enhance how you manage your energy:

- **Daily Energy Patterns:** Observe how your energy shifts throughout the day. When are you most energized? Which tasks consistently boost your energy, and which ones drain it? Sleep Habits: Reflect on the quality and consistency of your sleep. How does your sleep pattern influence your daily energy and focus? Physical Well-being: Consider how your exercise routine and dietary choices affect your stamina. Are there specific foods or habits that support or deplete your energy levels?
- **Stress Management:** Identify key stressors and how you typically respond to them. What coping strategies help you relax, reset, and recharge?
- **Mindfulness and Presence:** Practice staying present and focused in the moment. Are you taking intentional breaks to refocus and restore your energy during the day?
- **Work-Life Balance:** Reflect on your level of satisfaction with your work-life balance. Would setting clearer boundaries improve your well-being and energy management?
- **Social Connections:** Reflect on how different interactions influence your energy. Which relationships uplift and support you? Which ones tend to drain your energy? Focus on nurturing connections that encourage growth and positivity.

- **Goal Alignment:** Assess whether your daily activities align with your core goals and values. Are your current commitments moving you toward your long-term objectives, or do they require adjustment? Make intentional choices that reflect what matters most to you.
- **Learning and Growth:** Pay attention to how engaging with new ideas or skills affects your motivation and energy. What types of learning experiences leave you feeling inspired and energized?
- **Reflection and Adjustment:** Regularly review your energy levels and daily routines. What small changes could help you feel more balanced, focused, and productive? Be open to adjusting your habits as your needs evolve.

Consistently returning to these strategies will deepen your understanding of what fuels and drains your energy, empowering you to manage it more intentionally and effectively.

Circle of Empowerment Exercise

The Circle of Empowerment is a reflective tool designed to help you recognize what brings positivity into your life and what depletes your energy. By evaluating your relationships, environments, habits, and daily tasks, you can make more intentional choices that support your well-being and personal growth.

Instructions:

Begin by focusing on the Energizers section. List specific people, places, habits, and activities that uplift and energize you. Take time to reflect on these energizers, and consider how you can prioritize them in your daily life. Recognizing and reinforcing these positive influences will strengthen your ability to maintain energy and resilience.

Energizers

People Who Uplift You: Identify the individuals who consistently inspire, encourage, and support you. These are the people who leave you feeling more positive, empowered, and energized after spending time with them. Reflect on what makes these relationships meaningful and consider how you can nurture and prioritize them in your life.

- [Energizer 1]
- [Energizer 2]
- [Energizer 3]

Empowering Places: Identify the locations where you feel most at peace, motivated, and renewed. These might include specific rooms, outdoor spaces, or familiar spots like a favorite café or park. Reflect on what makes these places energizing for you and consider how you can incorporate more time in these environments to support your well-being.

- ❖ [Empowering Place 1]
- ❖ [Empowering Place 2]
- ❖ [Empowering Place 3]

Positive Habits: Identify the habits and routines that help you grow and feel your best. These are daily practices that support a positive mindset and overall well-being, such as exercising, journaling, or practicing gratitude. Reflect on how these habits contribute to your energy and consider ways to incorporate them more consistently into your life.

- ❖ [Positive Habit 1]
- ❖ [Positive Habit 2]
- ❖ [Positive Habit 3]

Energizing Tasks: Identify the tasks and activities that you genuinely look forward to—those that boost your motivation, focus, and overall energy. These might include working on a favorite hobby, learning something new, or organizing a space. Reflect on how these tasks make you feel and consider how to integrate more of them into your daily or weekly routine to maintain a sense of balance and fulfillment.

- ❖ [Energizing Task 1]
- ❖ [Energizing Task 2]

- ❖ [Energizing Task 3]

After identifying your energizers, turn your attention to the Drainers section. Here, list the individuals, places, habits, and tasks that consistently leave you feeling depleted, stressed, or overwhelmed. Reflecting on these drainers will help you recognize patterns that may be impacting your energy and well-being. Consider what boundaries or adjustments you might make to reduce their influence and protect your energy.

Drainers

Energy-Draining People: Identify individuals whose presence or interactions consistently leave you feeling stressed, discouraged, or emotionally exhausted. This reflection isn't about cutting people out of your life but about recognizing the effect they have on your energy. By becoming aware of these patterns, you empower yourself to manage these relationships in healthier ways—whether by setting clear boundaries, limiting time together, or adjusting expectations—to protect your well-being and peace of mind.

- ❖ [Drainer 1]
- ❖ [Drainer 2]
- ❖ [Drainer 3]

Draining Places: Identify the environments where you consistently feel anxious, uncomfortable, or unmotivated. Becoming aware of these spaces empowers you to set boundaries and limit time in places that deplete your energy or well-being.

- ❖ [Draining Place 1]
- ❖ [Draining Place 2]
- ❖ [Draining Place 3]

Negative Habits: Take time to reflect on behaviors that drain your energy or block your progress such as procrastination, excessive phone use, or lack of sleep. By recognizing these patterns, you create space for healthier habits that support your focus, well-being, and growth.

- ❖ [Negative Habit 1]
- ❖ [Negative Habit 2]
- ❖ [Negative Habit 3]

Draining Tasks: Identify tasks that consistently leave you feeling exhausted or overwhelmed even if they are necessary. Acknowledging these energy-draining responsibilities is the first step toward finding ways to manage or minimize their impact on your well-being and productivity.

- ❖ [Draining Task 1]
- ❖ [Draining Task 2]
- ❖ [Draining Task 3]

Patterns and Insights

After identifying your Energizers and Drainers, take a moment to reflect on the patterns that emerge:

Themes Among Uplifters: What common qualities, behaviors, or environments do the people and activities that uplift you share? Identifying these themes can help you intentionally seek more of what energizes and supports you.

Traits of Energy Drainers: Do you notice shared characteristics among the people, habits, or places that consistently drain your energy? Recognizing these patterns empowers you to set healthy boundaries and make meaningful adjustments that protect your well-being.

Alignment with Your Goals: How well do your surroundings, daily habits, and relationships support the direction you want to grow? Reflect on whether your current environment aligns with your vision and consider what changes might bring you closer to the life you want to create.

Reflection and Action

Once you recognize these patterns, take intentional steps to enhance your well-being:

- **Reduce Energy Drainers:** What specific actions can you take to minimize time spent with people, places, or habits that drain your energy? This might include setting firm boundaries, limiting interactions that leave you depleted, or rearranging your environment to better support your needs.

- **Choose Positive Spaces:** Which environments align with your goals and nourish your well-being? Make a conscious effort to spend more time in spaces that uplift and inspire you. Seek out places physical, mental, or emotional that energize and support your growth.
- **Cultivate Positive Habits:** What small, practical steps can you take to strengthen habits that boost your energy and momentum? Reflect on daily choices that move you away from draining behaviors and closer to actions aligned with your values and goals.

This reflective practice gives you a structured way to assess where your energy goes — and empowers you to take ownership of how and where you invest it.

Journal Prompt: "Illuminate Your Path"

Reflect on the practice of protecting your energy by exploring moments in your life that either uplift or drain you. In this journaling exercise, consider the activities, relationships, and environments that fuel or deplete your energy. By understanding these dynamics, you uncover valuable insights into the patterns and triggers that shape your energy both positively and negatively.

Getting Started

Begin by identifying specific moments when you felt energized or depleted. Reflect on the people, places, habits, or circumstances that influenced these experiences. Be honest about both the challenges that drain you and the experiences that uplift you. Recognizing both sides allows you to better understand your unique energy landscape.

Implementing Boundaries and Strategies

Write down clear strategies and boundaries you can apply daily to protect and sustain your energy. Consider how these actions align with your values and long-term goals. Then, envision a future where you consistently prioritize your well-being and reflect on the positive impact this would have on every part of your life.

Reflection Prompts to Illuminate Your Path

Harmony in Boundaries

Consider how setting boundaries creates a healthier balance between giving and receiving energy. How can clear boundaries help you maintain harmony in your relationships and daily activities? Reflect on how honoring your limits allows you to show up more fully and authentically for yourself and others.

Resilience Building

Think back to a time when saying "no" felt difficult but necessary. How did choosing to honor your limits help you build resilience and improve your well-being? Reflect on the strength and self-respect that emerged from protecting your energy, even when it was uncomfortable.

Empowerment Narrative

By valuing and protecting your energy, how has your sense of empowerment shifted? Reflect on the ways this awareness has changed your perspective and deepened your sense of self-worth. How has standing firm in your boundaries helped you trust yourself more?

Navigating Social Challenges

Recall an experience when prioritizing your well-being led to challenges in social situations. How did you handle these moments? What did you learn about yourself and others? Explore how facing these challenges contributed to your personal growth, resilience, and clarity about what you need.

Balancing Act

How do you currently find balance between protecting your energy and staying open to new opportunities? Reflect on what helps you remain receptive to growth while safeguarding your well-being. Consider the tools, habits, or mindset shifts that allow you to maintain this balance.

Internal Dialogues

Think of a time when saying “no” stirred up inner conflict or guilt. How did you work through those feelings? What did this experience teach you about self-care and emotional boundaries? Reflect on how navigating this internal dialogue shaped your ability to honor your needs without apology.

This journaling journey is about embracing both the empowering and challenging aspects of protecting your energy. It offers space for honest reflection, growth, and self-discovery. Let these prompts guide you toward deeper self-awareness, resilience, and strength reminding you that honoring your energy is an act of self-love and empowerment.

Why Protecting Your Energy Matters

It’s about crafting a life that truly aligns with who you are and what you value. Your energy is finite, and where you choose to invest it shapes your experiences, relationships, and overall well-being. By taking time to reflect, set boundaries, and nurture what uplifts you, you make an essential commitment to live with intention and meaning.

When you actively protect your energy, you acknowledge that your time, well-being, and mental health are worth prioritizing. This act of self-respect reinforces your inherent value, empowering you to make choices that honor your true needs and aspirations. Instead of being pulled in different directions by external demands, you become the architect of your own life capable of deciding where your energy flows.

Documenting your journey through journaling creates a space to revisit and recognize the progress you've made. This personal record of insights and reflections becomes a powerful reminder of the positive impact that protecting your energy has on your life. It can motivate you on difficult days and reinforce the significance of your choices, showing you how far you've come in honoring your personal boundaries.

In the end, safeguarding your energy empowers you to show up as your best self for both yourself and those you care about. It's an ongoing promise to nurture your strengths, pursue meaningful goals, and cultivate relationships that reflect your values. Let this journal stand as a testament to that commitment, illuminating your path to a more fulfilling, balanced, and purposeful life.

Chapter 4
Observing and Amending Your Circle

Let's talk about something essential, yet often overlooked: your circle. Your circle includes the people you surround yourself with, the habits you maintain, and the emotions you allow in. It's the environment you build around yourself every single day and here's the truth: that environment has a profound impact on your mental health, your energy, and your ability to thrive.

When you surround yourself with negativity whether it comes from people, unhealthy habits, or overwhelming emotions it weighs you down. It's like carrying invisible baggage that leaves you drained and stuck. But when you intentionally choose positivity cultivating habits and relationships that uplift and energize you it can transform your life in ways you may not have imagined.

Take something simple, like exercise. It doesn't have to be a marathon; even a quick daily walk or short workout can make a difference. That small habit becomes an anchor in your day, releasing feel-good endorphins, reducing stress, and boosting your mood. It's a small investment with big returns for both your body and mind.

In this chapter, we're going to explore how the choices you make about who and what you allow into your circle can either propel you forward or hold you back. By becoming intentional and thoughtful about your circle, you'll discover how much power you have to shape your path toward happiness and success.

Emotional Intelligence

Here's a powerful tool for navigating your circle: Emotional Intelligence. Think of it as a superpower for understanding yourself and the people around you. Emotional intelligence (or EQ) is the ability to recognize your own emotions, understand where they're coming from, and manage them in healthy ways. It's also about tuning into the emotions of others which allows you to build stronger, more meaningful connections.

So, what does emotional intelligence actually involve?

Self-awareness: This means understanding your own feelings knowing why you're upset, anxious, frustrated, or even happy. For example, if you're feeling stressed, being aware of it gives you the power to take steps to calm yourself or address the issue directly.

Empathy: Empathy is the ability to put yourself in someone else's shoes. It helps you understand why someone may be feeling a certain way and allows you to connect with them on a deeper, more compassionate level.

Emotion management: This is about handling emotions both your own and others in a way that avoids unnecessary conflict and supports healthy relationships. Emotion management also includes setting boundaries when someone or something drains your energy, protecting your well-being without guilt.

When you develop your emotional intelligence, you gain the tools to create a circle that supports you. You'll make better decisions about who belongs in your life and how to protect your energy from negativity.

Emotional Intelligence Exercise: "The Emotion Mapping Practice" This exercise is designed to help you deepen your self-awareness and empathy by identifying, understanding, and reflecting on emotions both your own and those of others. It combines mindfulness with intentional action to strengthen emotional intelligence in your daily interactions.

Step 1: Begin with a Self-Check-In (10 Minutes)

Find a quiet, comfortable space where you won't be interrupted. Gently close your eyes and take three slow, deep breaths to center yourself.

Reflect on the past 24 hours.

What emotions have you experienced?

When did you feel these emotions most intensely?

What triggered those emotions?

Write it down: Create a table like this in your journal:

Emotion	Situation	Trigger	Response	Confidence, calm down
Anxiety	Morning meeting	Fear of judgment	Nervous pacing	Confidence, calm down

Be specific, and focus on recognizing patterns in your triggers and responses.

Step 2: Reverse the Perspective (10 Minutes)

Think about a specific interaction you've had within the past day or week where emotions were involved. Take a moment to reflect and answer the following questions:

- What emotion do you think the other person was feeling? What do you believe triggered that emotion?
- How did their emotion influence their words, tone, or actions?
- Write it down: In your journal, describe the situation and your thoughts in detail. For example:

"During the team meeting, Jamie seemed frustrated. I think it was because their ideas weren't being heard. They crossed their arms and spoke more abruptly than usual."

Step 3: Emotion Mapping Reflection (5 Minutes)

Now, take a moment to compare your two reflections:

- How did your emotions shape your perspective during the interaction?
- Did you accurately recognize the other person's emotional state?
- What could you do differently in a similar situation to create better understanding or connection?

Step 4: Set a Daily Intention

Based on your reflections, choose *one* aspect of emotional intelligence to work on for the next 24 hours:

- **Self-awareness:** Pause to name your emotions during challenging moments. Empathy: Pay attention to nonverbal cues like tone, posture, or facial expressions in others.
- **Emotion management:** Practice responding to emotions calmly instead of reacting impulsively.
  Write down your intention: "Today, I will actively pause and identify my emotions before responding during stressful moments."

Step 5: Practice and Observe (All Day)

Throughout the day:

Pause briefly before or after significant interactions to notice emotions both your own and the other person's.

Reflect on how your intention influenced your responses and connection with others.

Step 6: End-of-Day Check-In (10 Minutes)

At the end of the day, return to your journal and reflect:

What emotions did I recognize in myself today?

Did I notice and better understand the emotions of others?

How did my actions today align with my intention to practice emotional intelligence? What would I like to improve or focus on tomorrow? By consistently practicing this exercise, you strengthen your ability to identify and manage emotions both your own and others in healthy, constructive ways. Over time, you'll notice stronger relationships, clearer communication, and deeper self-awareness.

Emotional Intelligence and Your Circle: Creating a Supportive Environment for Growth

Emotional intelligence is your compass for navigating the complexities of relationships, emotions, and everyday interactions. It helps you understand your own feelings, connect with others on a deeper level, and make intentional choices about how you respond to challenges. At its core, emotional intelligence is built on self-awareness, self-regulation, empathy, and relationship management essential skills that determine not only how well you understand yourself but also how effectively you engage with the world around you.

Yet, knowing yourself and mastering your emotions is only part of the equation. The next step is applying that awareness to your external world your circle. Your emotional intelligence shapes how you interpret social dynamics, set boundaries, and decide which relationships nourish your well-being and which ones deplete it. By taking an honest look at the people, habits, and influences you allow into your life, you can begin to create an environment that supports your growth and long-term fulfillment.

The Connection Between Emotional Intelligence and Your Relationships

The relationships in your life act as mirrors, reflecting aspects of your emotional intelligence back to you. The way you interact with others how you communicate, handle conflict, and express your needs is largely shaped by your level of emotional intelligence. In turn, the people in your circle can either reinforce healthy emotional patterns or trigger responses that disrupt your peace.

For example, individuals with high emotional intelligence tend to attract relationships built on mutual respect, deep understanding, and emotional safety. These relationships offer encouragement during difficult times, foster personal growth, and create space for vulnerability without judgment. On the other hand, low emotional intelligence often leads to relationships marked by miscommunication, emotional manipulation, or a lack of boundaries. When emotional awareness is lacking, it becomes easier to tolerate toxic dynamics, fall into people-pleasing patterns, or remain in relationships that no longer serve your highest good. By strengthening your emotional intelligence, you gain greater clarity to assess the quality of your relationships. Are your interactions with certain people leaving you drained or uplifted? Do you feel heard and valued, or do you find yourself constantly trying to prove your worth? Emotional intelligence helps you recognize whether your relationships support your growth or pull you away from your purpose.

Assessing the Emotional Climate of Your Circle

Every social circle has an emotional climate — a general feeling or energy that shapes how you feel when you engage with the people in it. Some circles are uplifting, filled with individuals who encourage self-reflection, celebrate progress, and offer genuine emotional support. Others may be draining, filled with individuals who are overly critical, dismissive, or emotionally unavailable.

To better understand the emotional climate of your circle, ask yourself these questions:

Who in my life brings out my best self? — Consider the people who inspire, challenge, and support you without judgment. Who drains my energy? Identify relationships that feel one-sided, emotionally exhausting, or misaligned with your values. Do I feel emotionally safe in my circle? Emotional safety is essential for healthy relationships. Do you feel like you can be fully yourself, or do you often feel like you're walking on eggshells? Are there patterns of emotional dysfunction in my relationships? Look for cycles of emotional manipulation, passive-aggressiveness, or unspoken resentment that may be undermining your well-being.

How do I contribute to the emotional dynamic of my circle? — Self-awareness is key. Are there ways your own emotional habits may be impacting the health of your relationships?

Taking stock of these factors helps you determine whether your circle is emotionally enriching or whether it needs intentional adjustments to support your growth and well-being.

Bridging Awareness and Action: The Next Step

Understanding emotional intelligence is only the beginning. Recognizing how your emotions shape your interactions — and how your relationships impact your well-being — is a crucial first step. However, awareness without action changes nothing. It's not enough to simply acknowledge how certain relationships or habits affect you — you must take intentional steps to ensure that your circle aligns with your growth, values, and purpose. This is where taking inventory of your circle becomes essential. Just as you might declutter your physical space to create a more peaceful and productive environment, evaluating the people, habits, and influences in your life allows you to clear emotional and mental clutter. By assessing what nurtures you versus what depletes you, you gain the clarity and power to design a support system that fuels your growth.

Let's explore why taking this inventory is one of the most transformative steps you can take toward creating a more intentional, empowered, and fulfilling life.

Why Taking Inventory of Your Circle Is Important

The people, habits, and environments you surround yourself with are not just passive elements of your life — they actively shape your mindset, emotions, and sense of purpose. Whether you realize it or not, your circle is influencing your thoughts, decisions, and overall well-being every day. Some relationships empower you — lifting you up and pushing you toward growth — while others subtly (or overtly) drain your energy, reinforce limiting beliefs, and hold you back from becoming your best self. Yet, we often allow our circles to form unconsciously, shaped by circumstances, routines, or past versions of ourselves. We maintain relationships out of habit, keep commitments that no longer serve us, and engage in behaviors that slowly chip away at our potential. Without intentional reflection, it's easy to stay stuck in patterns that feel familiar but ultimately limit our ability to thrive.

That's why taking inventory of your circle is a crucial practice — it allows you to assess the energy around you, redefine what you need, and make conscious choices about who and what belongs in your life moving forward.

This process isn't about judgment or cutting people off abruptly. Rather, it's about cultivating awareness. By shining a light on the dynamics that influence you, you can identify what's fueling your purpose and what's distracting you from it. It's an opportunity to realign with your values, set necessary boundaries, and cultivate a circle that truly supports your personal and professional growth.

Taking inventory is the first step toward reclaiming control over your environment — ensuring that the people and influences around you encourage your growth rather than stifle it.

1. Awareness Creates Change

You can't fix what you don't know.

Taking inventory helps you recognize the patterns, relationships, and habits that shape your daily life.

It shines a light on what's working for you — and what's holding you back.

This clarity is the first step toward meaningful change — because you can't create a better environment without knowing what needs improvement.

Your Circle Shapes Your Energy and Mindset

The people and habits in your circle can either:

- **Elevate you** — Positive influences inspire you, boost your energy, and encourage growth.
- **Drain you** — Negative influences leave you feeling exhausted, discouraged, or stuck.

  By taking inventory, you can identify what lifts you up and what weighs you down — allowing you to make intentional choices about where your energy goes and who gets access to it.

3. Emotional Health Depends on Boundaries

Without boundaries, you may find yourself:

Overcommitting to people or habits that drain your energy.

Feeling overwhelmed by negativity or constant conflict.

Losing sight of your own needs while focusing too much on others.

Taking stock of your circle allows you to recognize where boundaries need to be set — protecting your emotional well-being and creating space for growth.

4. Growth Requires Alignment

As you grow and evolve, your circle must align with your goals and values.

If you're working toward a healthier, more positive life, but your circle includes toxic relationships or draining habits, it becomes much harder to make progress.

By evaluating your circle, you can make intentional adjustments that align your environment with your aspirations.

5. You Are the Average of Your Circle

There's a saying: "You are the average of the five people you spend the most time with."

The attitudes, habits, and perspectives of those around you influence your mindset over time. If your circle is full of negativity, low motivation, or toxic dynamics, those patterns can seep into your own thinking and behavior. But when you surround yourself with supportive, ambitious, and positive people, it becomes easier to adopt those same qualities in your own life.

6. It's About Taking Control

Without reflection, it's easy to fall into autopilot, letting relationships, habits, or environments linger, even when they're no longer serving you.

Taking inventory puts you back in the driver's seat.

It gives you the power to choose who and what gets space in your life, allowing you to design a circle that supports your well-being and success.

The Outcome: Creating a Life That Reflects Your Growth

When you take inventory of your circle, you are doing more than just reflecting — you are actively shaping the quality of your life. Every person, habit, and environment you engage with plays a role in your well-being, your mindset, and your ability to thrive. This process is not just about removing negativity, it's about intentionally surrounding yourself with people and influences that uplift, inspire, and align with your vision for the future. It's about creating a space where your energy is protected, your values are honored, and your growth is continuously supported. By making the choice to evaluate your circle, you take ownership of your life in a powerful way. You are deciding that your energy is worth protecting, your goals are worth prioritizing, and your happiness is worth cultivating. It may not always be easy, change rarely is, but every intentional shift, every thoughtful boundary, and every conscious decision to align with what truly serves you brings you closer to the best version of yourself.

This is a defining moment — one where you reclaim control, set the stage for deeper fulfillment, and step forward with clarity and confidence. By taking inventory, you are not just adjusting your circle you are designing a life that reflects your highest potential, one intentional choice at a time. And that is a powerful step toward the life you deserve.

Exercise: Taking Inventory of Your Circle

Let's take a moment for some self-reflection. Think about your circle — the people, habits, emotions, and situations that shape your daily life. In your journal (or even on a piece of paper), create two lists:

What lifts you up — These are the people, habits, and experiences that bring you joy, calm, and energy.

What brings you down — These are the things that drain you, stress you out, or hold you back. Be honest with yourself — this isn't about judgment; it's about understanding. Recognizing what's working and what's not is the first step toward making changes that align with your well-being.

The Art of Repositioning

Now that you have a clearer picture of what your circle looks like, let's talk about repositioning. Think of it as rearranging a puzzle to create an image that better reflects who you are and where you want to go.

- **Repositioning people** — Take a closer look at the relationships in your life. Who uplifts you and makes you feel supported? Who drains your energy? This isn't about cutting people out entirely (unless necessary), but about setting boundaries and deciding how much space certain people should take up in your life.

- **Repositioning activities** — Reflect on how you spend your time. Are there activities that bring you joy and fulfillment? Are there routines that no longer serve you? Shift your focus to what nourishes your body and mind, and let go of what doesn't.
- **Repositioning behaviors** — What patterns are holding you back? Maybe it's saying "yes" to everything and feeling overwhelmed. Or maybe it's staying up too late and struggling to get through the next day. Whatever it is, identify those behaviors and commit to changing them step by step.

Repositioning is about taking control of your environment so it fully supports your growth, well-being, and happiness.

Cultivating Healthy Habits: Small Shifts, Lasting Impact

Your habits are at the core of your circle. They are the routines that shape your days and, ultimately, your life. The way you move through each day, how you nourish your body, how you speak to yourself, and how you spend your time — determines whether you are building a foundation that supports your purpose or one that slowly pulls you away from it.

The good news? Small changes, done consistently, lead to big results. You don't need a drastic overhaul, just intentional, sustainable shifts.

Start simple. Maybe you commit to five minutes of meditation each morning to cultivate mindfulness, swap an unhealthy snack for a nourishing option, or replace mindless scrolling on social media with reading something that expands your perspective. Small choices, repeated daily, have the power to rewire your habits and create a ripple effect of positive change throughout your life.

The key is to begin where you are and build from there. Even the smallest effort, when done consistently, strengthens your ability to maintain momentum and momentum is what leads to lasting change.

The Power of Micro-Habits

One of the biggest mistakes people make when trying to build new habits is attempting a complete transformation overnight. This often leads to burnout, frustration, and abandoning the effort before any real progress takes root. Instead, focus on micro-habits—small, manageable actions that fit naturally into your existing routines. These tiny steps build momentum and, over time, lead to lasting change. For example:

If you want to increase your physical activity, start with five minutes of stretching instead of committing to an hour-long workout right away.

If you want to practice gratitude, begin by writing down one thing you’re thankful for each morning, rather than feeling pressured to fill pages with reflections. If you want to improve your focus, take two minutes for deep breathing before starting a task, instead of forcing yourself into rigid productivity routines.

These small shifts may seem insignificant at first, but over time, they compound into meaningful change. The consistency of your actions matters far more than their intensity.

Focus on Consistency Over Perfection

Perfection is not the goal—progress is. It's better to take small, steady steps than to pursue an all-or-nothing approach that leads to burnout. If you miss a day or slip back into an old habit, don't let it derail you. What matters most is that you return to your intention without guilt or self-judgment. Habits are built through repetition, not flawless execution.

Think of your habits as seeds. At first, they may seem small and insignificant, but with patience, care, and daily attention, they grow into something strong and lasting. The way you shape your habits shapes your future. So, start with one simple change today your future self will thank you.

Amending Your Circle: Aligning Your Relationships with Your Growth Lastly, let's talk about the people in your circle. Relationships are among the most powerful influences in your life—they can either elevate you toward your highest potential or drain your energy and keep you stuck in patterns that no longer serve you. If you often feel exhausted, unappreciated, or unsupported in certain relationships, it may be time to reevaluate their place in your life.

Amending your circle doesn't always mean cutting people off completely. Instead, it's about redefining how you engage with them. Some relationships may require firmer boundaries, limiting how much time and energy you invest. Others may need a shift in expectations—recognizing that not everyone can meet you at the depth you desire. And sometimes, you may realize that certain connections have simply run their course, and letting them go becomes an act of self-preservation, not cruelty.

Setting boundaries is an act of self-respect. It allows you to protect your emotional well-being while still creating space for healthy connections. This might mean having honest conversations about your needs, reducing time spent in draining interactions, or adjusting the level of emotional investment you give to one-sided relationships. Remember, boundaries are not about shutting people out—they're about ensuring your energy is spent in ways that align with your growth. At the same time, amending your circle also means making room for relationships that uplift, encourage, and respect you. Seek out people who inspire you, challenge you in meaningful ways, and celebrate your progress. Surround yourself with those who see your potential and support your vision for the future. If you feel a lack of meaningful connections, consider joining new communities, connecting with like-minded individuals, or deepening bonds with people who genuinely align with your values.

Above all, remember that this is your journey. Your circle isn't fixed it will evolve as you do. People change, priorities shift, and as you grow, your needs and boundaries may look different than they once did. Celebrate every small victory in refining your relationships, and give yourself permission to reassess and adjust when necessary. Life is dynamic, and curating a circle that nurtures your well-being is an ongoing process.

Final Thoughts: Choosing Your Circle with Intention

Every choice you make about your circle is a step toward creating a life that reflects both who you are and who you want to become. Your relationships are more than social connections they are energetic exchanges that shape your mindset, influence your habits, and affect your overall well-being.

By observing, adjusting, and intentionally shaping your circle, you build a foundation for growth, happiness, and success. It's not about having the most people around you—it's about having the right people. The ones who support you, challenge you to grow, and genuinely care about your journey.

Protect your energy. Choose connections that nourish your spirit. And, most importantly, trust yourself to recognize which relationships align with your purpose and which may need to shift. As you continue to grow, your circle should evolve with you, reflecting the life and values you are building.

You’ve got this.

Chapter 5
Unlocking Your Gifts and Talents

Each of us holds unique abilities—gifts and talents that, when discovered, nurtured, and shared, lead to a life of purpose and fulfillment. These gifts are the threads that weave together our individuality and allow us to contribute meaningfully to the world around us. This chapter, Unlocking Your

Gifts, is an invitation to explore those unique traits within yourself, develop them fully, and integrate them into your daily life in ways that elevate not only your personal experience but also inspire and uplift others.

Discovering your gifts isn't only about self-improvement—it's about stepping into your potential and becoming a source of light for those around you. It's about turning inward to uncover what makes you unique and learning how to let that uniqueness shine. But this journey isn't always easy. It requires self-reflection, patience, and a willingness to push past fear and self-doubt.

We'll begin by exploring Self-Discovery of Gifts and Talents—a journey of looking within to identify what brings you joy, excitement, and purpose. From there, we'll examine The Power of External Reflection to understand how the world around us often reveals aspects of our abilities we may overlook.

Once your talents come into focus, we'll discuss Nurturing and Developing Your Talents, transforming raw potential into refined skills through deliberate practice and dedication. Along the way, we'll confront Overcoming Impostor Syndrome and Self-Doubt, giving you tools to move beyond mental barriers that may hold you back. Next, we'll explore Integrating Talents into Personal and Professional Life, so your gifts become an active, vibrant part of your everyday experience. Finally, we'll look at The Impact of

Sharing Your Gifts with the World—the ultimate fulfillment of this journey, where your talents become a force for connection, inspiration, and change.

Each section includes reflective exercises designed to help you engage with the material, apply it to your life, and take actionable steps toward unlocking your potential. As you move through this chapter, remember: your talents are not just for you. They are meant to be shared, creating ripples of positivity and growth that extend far beyond yourself. Self-Discovery of Gifts and Talents Discovering your gifts is like unearthing treasures hidden deep within some waiting just beneath the surface, others buried under years of doubt, fear, or external expectations. These talents are not just skills; they are the essence of what makes you uniquely you, shaping your passions, perspectives, and the value you bring to the world.

Some gifts are obvious, showing up early in life as natural talents or deeply rooted interests. Others reveal themselves over time—through experiences, challenges, and moments of inspiration that awaken something inside you. Yet in a world that often equates talent with external achievement, it's easy to overlook or undervalue the gifts that truly make you special. You may have dismissed your creativity because it doesn't fit a traditional career path, or ignored your ability to connect deeply with others because it isn't easily measured. But your gifts don't need validation to be real. They exist whether or not the world recognizes them, and their true power emerges when you choose to acknowledge and nurture them.

This section is about guiding you inward—beyond doubt and self-limiting beliefs—to rediscover the abilities that have always been a part of you. It's about recognizing both the grand and subtle ways you contribute to the world—whether through artistry, leadership, problem-solving, empathy, or innovation. No matter how big or small, every gift holds purpose. Embracing them is not just an act of self-acceptance—it's a step toward living with greater joy, impact, and authenticity.

The Essence of Self-Discovery

Self-discovery of your gifts and talents is more than identifying what you're good at—it's about uncovering what sparks your soul and makes you feel truly alive. When you tap into those activities, moments, or strengths that resonate deeply, you connect with the essence of who you are. It's not just about skills; it's about the light within you that shines brightest when you're doing something meaningful and aligned with your natural abilities.

But this kind of discovery requires intention. It calls for slowing down, reflecting, and being honest with yourself about what brings you joy, where you naturally excel, and what you may have overlooked or undervalued within yourself.

Reflective Questions and Prompts

To begin uncovering your gifts, consider these questions: When do you feel most alive? Reflect on the moments when time seems to disappear and you feel fully engaged—those experiences that light you up from within.

What comes naturally to you? These are the things that feel effortless—so natural that you might overlook them as talents simply because they require little thought or struggle.

What did you love as a child? Childhood interests often reflect our purest passions, untouched by the pressures and expectations that come with adulthood.

What do others consistently compliment you on? Sometimes, the world sees strengths in us that we have yet to fully recognize or embrace.

Self-Assessment Exercises

Here are some practical steps to help you pinpoint your talents:

- **Skills Inventory:** Make a list of every skill or ability you possess—even those that seem minor or insignificant. Often, hidden gems emerge when you take the time to acknowledge everything, you're capable of.
- **Feedback Collection:** Ask trusted friends, family, or colleagues to share what they see as your strengths. Their

insights might surprise you and reveal gifts you've overlooked.

- **Passion Project Reflection:** Reflect on any projects, hobbies, or activities you've pursued purely for enjoyment. What drew you to them? What aspects of those experiences made you feel alive and engaged?

Navigating the Landscape of Self-Discovery

Remember, this isn't about rushing to a conclusion it's about exploration. Your talents and gifts will evolve as you do, revealing new dimensions over time. Approach this process with patience and curiosity, and celebrate every insight as a meaningful step toward a fuller understanding of yourself. As you uncover your talents, know that they are not meant solely for your benefit. They represent your unique contribution to the world a way to enrich your own life while also making a meaningful difference in the lives of others.

This is just the beginning of our exploration. As we move forward, we'll begin looking outward to see how the people and world around us reflect our abilities, offering deeper insight into who we are. So, let's step into the power of external reflection.

The Power of External Reflection

While the journey of self-discovery begins within, the world around us serves as a mirror, reflecting dimensions of our talents we may not easily see on our own. Feedback from others, their responses to us, and the opportunities we encounter all offer valuable clues about the gifts we carry. External reflection helps us uncover hidden strengths, validate our abilities, and gain new perspectives on how we can grow and contribute.

Understanding External Reflection

External reflection is the process of actively engaging with feedback, insights, and observations from the people and environments around you. It's about noticing what the world reflects back—what others see in your actions, your work, and your interactions. This feedback doesn't define you, but it can illuminate aspects of your talents you might have overlooked or undervalued.

This process requires an open mind and heart. Sometimes, feedback challenges our self-perception or reveals areas where we can grow. Embracing these insights with a growth mindset can propel you forward, offering a deeper understanding of your unique abilities.

The Art of Receiving Feedback

Feedback is a powerful tool, but receiving it isn't always easy. Learning to embrace feedback involves:

Distinguishing constructive feedback from opinion: Constructive feedback offers actionable insights that support your growth.

Opinions, while valid, may not always align with your goals or values—and that's okay.

Listening for patterns: When multiple people highlight the same strengths or suggest similar areas for improvement, pay attention. These patterns can reveal important truths about your abilities and opportunities for growth.

Focusing on growth: Feedback isn't about judgment, it's an opportunity to refine and develop your talents. Approaching feedback with a growth mindset allows you to use it as a tool for learning and personal evolution.

Strategies for Seeking Constructive Feedback

To get the most out of external reflection, approach feedback with intention:

- **Be specific in your requests:** Instead of asking, "What do you think of my work?" try asking, "How can I improve this aspect of my project?" Clear, focused questions invite more actionable and helpful responses.
- **Seek diverse perspectives:** Different people will notice different strengths and areas for growth. Reach out to friends, mentors, colleagues, and even clients to gain well-rounded feedback.

- **Create a safe space for honesty:** Let people know you value their input and are open to constructive feedback without judgment. When others feel safe to be honest, their insights become far more meaningful and helpful.

The Role of Mentors and Communities

Mentors and communities of practice are invaluable sources of external reflection. Mentors offer guidance, inspiration, and personalized feedback shaped by their experience. Communities—whether online or in person—create a network of like-minded individuals who challenge, support, and encourage you to grow.

Engaging with these groups allows you to see your talents in action, connect them to broader goals, and identify opportunities to strengthen and refine them further.

Navigating Challenges Not all feedback will be useful, and some may even be unkind. That's why it's essential to filter feedback keeping what serves you and letting go of what doesn't. Trust your intuition, and focus on insights that align with your values and goals.

Reflection Exercise: Feedback and Growth

Take time to gather feedback from three people who know you well. Ask them to identify:

- Your top three strengths.

- One area where you could improve or grow.
- A moment when they've seen you at your best.

Compare their answers and reflect on common themes. How do these insights align with your own self-perception? Are there new strengths or areas for growth that surprise you?

External reflection is a powerful tool for unlocking the full potential of your talents. By embracing feedback, seeking mentors, and engaging with supportive communities, you gain a well-rounded view of your abilities and a clearer path for growth.

Next, we'll take these insights and move into the heart of development—nurturing and refining your talents into skills that truly shine.

Nurturing and Developing Your Talents

Discovering your talents is only the beginning. True transformation happens when you commit time and effort to developing those raw abilities into refined skills. Nurturing your talents takes consistent practice, ongoing learning, and a commitment to growth but the results can be life-changing.

The Foundation of Talent Development

❖ Talent alone is not enough. To truly thrive, you must intentionally develop your abilities by setting clear goals and committing to consistent growth. Success requires more than **raw skill** — it demands ongoing effort and discipline.

- Development is an active, evolving process that includes:
- **Practice** — Purposeful, focused effort to sharpen and refine your skills.
- **Learning** — Continuously seeking new knowledge, feedback, and resources to deepen your expertise.
- **Reflection** — Regularly evaluating your progress, identifying areas for improvement, and adjusting your approach. When you embrace this ongoing process, you not only strengthen your abilities but also build unshakable confidence in your potential.

Setting Goals and Creating a Development Plan

To effectively nurture your talents, you need a clear and focused approach that sets you up for success. Here's how to begin:

- **Identify specific areas for growth** — Choose one or two talents to prioritize at first, so you can direct your energy where it will have the most impact.
- **Set SMART goals** — Make sure your goals are Specific, Measurable, Achievable, Relevant, and Time-bound. For example: "Improve my public speaking by practicing weekly and attending a workshop within the next three months."

- **Break it down into actionable steps** — Outline the concrete actions you'll take and the resources you'll need, such as books, courses, or mentors who can guide you along the way. By following these steps, you create a clear roadmap for growth and give yourself the structure needed to move from intention to achievement.

Embracing a Growth Mindset

Talent development thrives on a growth mindset — the belief that effort, persistence, and practice can continually improve your abilities. Embracing this mindset allows you to see challenges as opportunities to learn and grow, rather than as roadblocks to success. It also builds resilience in the face of setbacks, helping you stay focused on progress over perfection.

The Role of Practice and Learning

Deliberate practice is the foundation of true growth. It's not just about repetition but about intentional effort—pushing your limits and refining your skills with purpose. To accelerate your development, pair practice with continuous learning through workshops, online courses, and mentorship. These resources provide fresh insights and help you expand your expertise.

Overcoming Challenges in Development

Every growth journey comes with obstacles, from stagnation to self-doubt. To stay on track, try these strategies:

Introduce variety Experiment with different techniques and approaches to keep your practice dynamic and engaging.

Seek feedback Regular check-ins with mentors or peers provide guidance, reveal blind spots, and reignite momentum. Celebrate milestones Acknowledge even small victories to reinforce motivation and sustain long-term commitment.

By actively nurturing your talents, you transform potential into mastery. This process requires dedication, but the rewards are profound greater confidence, deeper fulfillment, and a lasting impact.

Now, let's tackle one of the biggest barriers to growth: impostor syndrome and self-doubt. In the next section, we'll explore how to break free from these mental roadblocks and fully embrace your potential.

Overcoming Impostor Syndrome and Self-Doubt

Even as we nurture and refine our talents, many of us face a persistent challenge: the feeling of not being "good enough." Impostor syndrome and self-doubt often creep in, convincing us that our achievements are mere luck or that we're not as capable as others believe.

But here's the truth: these feelings are not a reflection of your abilities — they are a reflection of fear.

This section is about recognizing those doubts, reframing them, and building the confidence to fully own your talents. When you learn to move beyond these mental barriers, you open the door to growth, self-belief, and the courage to embrace your unique gifts.

Understanding Impostor Syndrome and Self-Doubt

Impostor syndrome is that persistent, nagging feeling that you're a fraud — that your achievements aren't truly deserved and that it's only a matter of time before you're "found out." Self-doubt, on the other hand, is the quiet voice questioning your abilities, decisions, or worth. Both are often fueled by fear of failure, perfectionism, and constant comparison to others.

These feelings are more common than you think — even among highly accomplished people. The key isn't to eliminate them completely, but to recognize them for what they are: temporary hurdles, not permanent truths.

Recognizing Triggers

One of the first steps in overcoming impostor syndrome and self-doubt is identifying what triggers them. Recognizing these patterns helps you prepare for moments when those feelings may surface.

Common triggers include:

- **Starting a new challenge or role** — Stepping into unfamiliar territory can amplify feelings of inadequacy.
- **Receiving criticism or feedback** — Even constructive input can sometimes be misinterpreted as confirmation of your doubts.
- **Comparing yourself to others in your field** — Measuring your progress against someone else's journey can fuel insecurity.
- **Achieving success that feels "too big" or sudden** — Rapid growth or recognition may trigger fears of being "found out."
- Once you understand what sparks these feelings, you can equip yourself to face them directly, rather than letting them hold you back.

Reframing Negative Thoughts or Negative Self-Talk

- Our inner dialogue holds immense power. When impostor syndrome or self-doubt creeps in, it's essential to challenge those negative thoughts before they take hold. Here are three strategies to help you reframe and reclaim your mindset: **Recognize the voice of self-doubt** — When you catch yourself thinking, "I'm not good enough," pause and acknowledge that this is self-doubt speaking — not reality.

- **Counter with evidence** — Remind yourself of past successes, skills you've built, and obstacles you've overcome. Reflecting on what you've already achieved reinforces the truth of your capabilities.
- **Adopt a growth mindset** — Instead of seeing setbacks as proof of inadequacy, choose to view them as opportunities to learn, improve, and grow stronger.

Building a Supportive Network

Surrounding yourself with supportive people makes all the difference. A strong network of friends, mentors, and peers offers:

- Encouragement when you feel unsure.
- Constructive feedback that helps you grow.
- Affirmation of your talents and worth.

Lean on this network during moments of doubt, and don't hesitate to share your feelings—chances are, they're more common than you think.

Practicing Self-Compassion

When you struggle with self-doubt, treat yourself the way you would treat a friend. Would you criticize a friend for trying something new or making a mistake? Of course not. You would offer encouragement, kindness, and understanding. Practice giving yourself the same compassion.

Reflective Exercise: Rewriting the Narrative

Think of a recent moment when you felt like an impostor or doubted your abilities. Take a few minutes to write down:

- What happened.
- How you felt.
- The thoughts that ran through your mind.

Now, rewrite that experience from a perspective of strength and growth. Focus on the effort, skills, and resilience you brought to the situation. Reflect on what you learned and how it has prepared you for future challenges

Moving Forward with Confidence

Impostor syndrome and self-doubt may never disappear completely, but with practice, you can quiet them and replace them with self-belief. Remember, you are not alone—and your feelings are not facts. Trust in the work you've done, the talents you've cultivated, and the value you offer.

With a stronger sense of confidence, it's time to move forward and integrate your talents into both your personal and professional life, making them an active, vibrant part of your everyday experience.

Integrating Talents into Personal and Professional Life

Recognizing and nurturing your talents is one thing—but bringing them to life in your daily world is another. True integration means weaving your gifts into every part of your life until they become a natural and fulfilling expression of who you are both personally and professionally.

When you consciously incorporate your talents into the way you live and work, you align with your authentic self. This alignment not only fuels personal fulfillment and professional success but also deepens your connection to purpose.

Strategies for Personal Integration

Pursue Passion Projects: Dedicate time to activities that let your talents shine. Whether it's painting, volunteering, writing, or anything that excites you, passion projects spark joy and create a deep sense of fulfillment.

Incorporate Talents into Daily Life:

Find small, meaningful ways to use your abilities every day. If you're naturally organized, plan a family event or streamline your home to create more ease and flow.

Create Rituals Around Your Talents:

Turn your talents into a regular part of your routine. If you love to write, try journaling each morning. If creativity speaks to you, cook meals that allow you to experiment and express yourself.

Strategies for Professional Integration

- **Align Your Role with Your Strengths:** Identify and pursue opportunities within your job that allow you to leverage your natural talents. For instance, if public speaking is one of your strengths, proactively volunteer to lead presentations or facilitate meetings.
- **Develop New Skills:** Continually expand your abilities by actively seeking training programs, mentorship opportunities, or collaborative projects that push you beyond your current capabilities. Engaging in these growth-oriented activities builds confidence and increases your professional versatility.
- **Share Your Talents:** Showcase your strengths and simultaneously contribute positively to your workplace by mentoring colleagues, facilitating workshops, or openly sharing your ideas during team discussions. By doing this, you elevate both your visibility and the success of those around you.

Overcoming Integration Challenges

Successfully integrating your talents into your professional life often means overcoming obstacles such as time constraints, unsupportive work environments, or the fear of stepping out of your comfort zone. Consider these approaches to address common barriers:

- Prioritize small, manageable steps that fit realistically into your current schedule.
- Advocate confidently for the value you bring to your organization by clearly communicating how your strengths contribute positively to team and organizational goals.
- Maintain your motivation by regularly reminding yourself of the long-term benefits of living authentically and fully utilizing your gifts.

Reflective Exercise: Integration Strategy

Choose one of your talents and brainstorm three ways to incorporate it into your personal life, as well as three ways you could utilize it professionally. Select one of these ideas and commit to implementing it this week. Afterward, reflect on the experience: What worked well? What could you improve next time? When you intentionally integrate your talents into everyday life, you allow your unique gifts to blossom fully. This enriches not only your own journey but also positively influences those around you. With your gifts now in full bloom, you're prepared to move forward into the final and most impactful phase of this journey: sharing your talents with the world.

Let's explore how openly sharing your unique abilities can create powerful ripples of inspiration and growth, reaching far beyond yourself.

The Impact of Sharing Your Gifts with the World

Discovering and developing your talents is a deeply fulfilling journey, but their true power lies in sharing them. Your abilities are not just personal assets—they have the potential to inspire, uplift, and drive meaningful change in the lives of others. When you share your gifts, your growth extends beyond yourself, becoming a catalyst for collective progress.

In this section, we'll explore the lasting impact of sharing your talents and provide practical strategies to help you do so with confidence and purpose. Why Sharing Matters: The Power of Contribution Sharing your gifts does more than highlight your abilities—it forges connections, nurtures growth, and leaves a lasting impact. Your talents, skills, and perspectives are not meant to remain hidden; they are meant to be expressed, experienced, and shared in ways that enrich both your life and the lives of others.

Too often, we hesitate to share out of fear—fear of judgment, fear that our contributions won't be "enough," or fear that what we offer won't make a difference. But sharing is not about perfection; it's about presence, generosity, and the courage to contribute authentically. When you share your gifts, you don't merely put something into the world—you shape it. You create inspiration, foster connections, and leave an imprint that extends far beyond yourself.

The Impact of Sharing Your Gifts

It Inspires Others – When you share your talents, you unconsciously encourage others to embrace and explore their own. Your courage to express yourself ignites creativity in others, showing them what's possible when they, too, step into their strengths.

It Builds Community – Every contribution, no matter how small, strengthens the fabric of the spaces you inhabit—your workplace, neighborhood, social circles, and beyond. Your willingness to share fosters collaboration, deepens relationships, and cultivates a sense of belonging.

It Fulfills Your Purpose – Gifts that remain unshared never reach their full potential. The act of sharing allows your talents to take shape in the world, infusing meaning into your efforts and creating a legacy that extends beyond the moment. Your strengths were never meant to be kept to yourself—they are meant to be used, appreciated, and woven into the greater collective.

Your perspective, creativity, and skills hold immense value—not just for you, but for those around you. Whether you share through your work, your words, your art, or simply your presence, you are making a difference. By choosing to share, you affirm the worth of your gifts, strengthen the connections around you, and contribute to a world that flourishes through the collective expression of individual strengths.

Ways to Share Your Talents

Sharing your talents doesn't have to be grand or public. Start small and stay authentic, focusing on the joy and connection it brings.

1. **Community Involvement**

Volunteer your skills for local projects or charitable organizations. Offer your expertise through teaching or mentorship. Participate in events that align with your talents, such as art fairs, public speaking engagements, or local initiatives.

2. Professional Contributions

Mentor colleagues or lead a team project that leverages your strengths.

Create workshops, presentations, or training sessions to share your knowledge.

Introduce innovative solutions in your workplace that draw on your expertise and perspective.

3. Online Platforms

Use social media, blogs, or videos to share your experiences and insights.

Join online communities where your talents contribute to discussions or collaborative projects.

Offer virtual workshops or tutorials to reach a global audience.

The Benefits of Sharing Your Gifts: How Contribution Transforms You and Others

When you share your talents, the impact is far greater than you may realize. Sharing is not just about giving—it's about growing, connecting, and inspiring. It strengthens your confidence, deepens your relationships, and creates a ripple effect that extends beyond what you can see. The gifts you bring to the world—whether through creativity, leadership, knowledge, or support—hold the power to create meaningful change, not just for others, but for yourself as well.

Personal Growth: Sharpening Your Skills and Expanding Your Potential

Sharing your talents challenges you to refine and elevate them. When you teach, create, or contribute in a meaningful way, you push yourself to grow. You explore new perspectives, deepen your understanding, and develop greater confidence in your abilities. Stepping outside your comfort zone to share your knowledge or creations may feel vulnerable at first, but in doing so, you build resilience, courage, and a stronger sense of self. Each time you share, you open yourself to feedback, collaboration, and new opportunities for learning—all of which fuel both personal and professional growth.

Connection: Building Meaningful Relationships and Community

When you share your gifts, you naturally attract like-minded individuals who resonate with your energy, values, and passions. Whether in your personal life, workplace, or creative endeavors, sharing helps you forge authentic connections. It allows you to build a network of support, inspiration, and collaboration—one that fosters mutual growth. These relationships create a sense of belonging, reminding you that you are not alone on your journey. By sharing, you cultivate spaces where others feel seen, heard, and valued, strengthening bonds that elevate everyone involved.

Inspiration: Igniting Possibility in Others Your willingness to share can be the spark that helps someone recognize their own potential. When you step forward and use your talents boldly, you silently encourage others to do the same. You never know who might be watching, learning, or finding courage through your journey. Your story, your struggles, and your growth hold power. They show others what is possible and inspire them to embrace their own gifts with confidence. In this way, sharing your talents creates a ripple effect of inspiration, multiplying positivity, creativity, and transformation in ways you may never fully witness. At its core, sharing is a cycle of growth, connection, and contribution. The more you share, the more you grow. The more you grow, the greater your impact. And the greater your impact, the more you inspire those around you to do the same. Your gifts are not meant to stay hidden—they are meant to be seen, felt, and shared in a way that brings light both to yourself and to the world.

Overcoming the Fear of Sharing

Sharing your talents can feel vulnerable—it places you in the spotlight and exposes you to feedback or criticism. To overcome these fears:

- **Focus on value:** Remember that sharing is about offering value to others, not about perfection.

- **Start small:** Share with a trusted friend or small group before expanding to larger audiences.
- **Embrace feedback:** Use constructive feedback as a tool for growth and improvement.

Reflective Exercise: Sharing Plan

Take a moment to reflect on your talents and how they can positively impact others. Write down: A specific talent you wish to share. One way you can offer it to your community, workplace, or online. A step-by-step plan to put this into action within the next month. After sharing, reflect on the experience:

- How did it feel?
- What was the response?
- What did you learn?

The Ripple Effect of Sharing: How Your Gifts Create a Lasting Impact

Sharing your talents is not just an individual act; it's an offering to the world, a contribution to something larger than yourself. The gifts you possess—whether big or small—hold the power to inspire, heal, and create transformation in ways you may never fully realize. A single word of encouragement, a piece of wisdom shared at the right moment, or a creative expression released into the world can spark change in someone else's journey, setting off a ripple effect of growth and possibility.

The ripple effect of sharing your gifts reaches far beyond what you can imagine. You may inspire someone to take the first step toward their dreams, offer comfort to someone who needs to hear your story, or provide a solution that helps a community overcome a challenge. When you show up authentically and share your essence with the world, you become a beacon of light—igniting courage, creativity, and hope in others.

But sharing is not about perfection. It's about presence and intention. Too often, we hesitate to share our gifts because we fear they are not polished enough, significant enough, or worthy of recognition. Yet, the true power of contribution lies not in flawlessness but in authenticity. A heartfelt effort, an honest expression, or a simple act of kindness carries more meaning than something curated for approval. The world doesn't need another perfect creation—it needs you, in your fullest and most honest form.

As you embrace this final phase of unlocking your gifts, remember that your impact is not measured by scale, but by sincerity. Whether you inspire one person or many, whether your work is seen or unseen, your willingness to share is what matters. Each time you offer your gifts to the world, you set new ripples in motion—ripples that have the potential to touch lives, shift perspectives, and create lasting change. So step forward, embrace your gifts, and trust that what you share will make a difference in ways you may never see.

Reflective Exercises for Further Exploration

To deepen your engagement with the concepts in this chapter, try one or more of the following exercises:

- **Daily Reflection on Talents**
  For one week, take time each evening to reflect on how you used your talents that day. Write about moments when you felt they made a positive impact, whether on yourself or others.
- **Feedback Loop**
  After sharing your talents in a specific way, ask those you interacted with for feedback. Reflect on their responses and think about how you might refine your approach.
- **Visioning Exercise**
  Imagine what your life would look like in five years if you consistently shared and honed your talents. What changes would you see in yourself, your community, and your professional life?

Closing Thoughts

The journey of discovering, developing, and sharing your talents is one of the most fulfilling paths you can take. It's not only about personal growth but also about contributing to the world in meaningful ways. Every talent, whether simple or extraordinary, has the potential to make a difference.

As we conclude this chapter, remember: your gifts are a light meant to shine. By sharing them, you create connections, inspire others, and leave a legacy of impact that reaches far beyond yourself.

Next, we move into the next natural step of this journey: "Reciprocation through Recognition." In the following chapter, we'll explore how celebrating and acknowledging the talents of others fosters a culture of mutual respect, growth, and shared success. Let's dive into this powerful practice and discover how recognizing others' contributions can elevate not only them but also your own journey.

Chapter 6
Reignite Your Purpose

Understanding Purpose: Defining Purpose

Purpose is the guiding force that aligns your inner essence with your outward actions—a dynamic expression of authenticity, confidence, and impact. It's not about seeking external validation or conforming to societal expectations; rather, it's a deep connection to what fuels you from within. Your purpose reflects in your decisions, interactions, and contributions, creating a sense of fulfillment that inspires those around you.

Think of purpose as a beacon, like a lighthouse guiding ships toward their destination. It's steady, unwavering, and uniquely yours. Even when challenges arise, your purpose remains constant if nurtured from within. It's not about perfection, but about embracing your journey as part of what makes you whole and impactful.

Many of us are conditioned to suppress our true purpose due to societal norms or personal doubts. Reigniting your purpose is an act of liberation—an intentional return to what drives you, fuels you, and makes you come alive.

Purpose is not a fixed destination but an evolving force, shifting as you grow, learn, and experience life. There may be times when your purpose feels unclear, buried under responsibilities, disappointments, or the expectations of others. But this doesn't mean it has disappeared; rather, it's an invitation to pause, reflect, and reconnect. Just as fire needs oxygen to burn, your purpose needs space—time to be explored, understood, and realigned with the person you are becoming. Reigniting your purpose begins with curiosity and self-inquiry. What excites you? What moments in your life have felt most meaningful? Purpose often reveals itself in the spaces where passion meets service—where what you love intersects with how you can contribute to the world around you. It may manifest through your career, relationships, creative pursuits, or personal growth, but at its core, it is always about connection—to yourself, to others, and to something greater than yourself.

Most importantly, embracing your purpose requires courage. It demands that you step beyond your comfort zone, challenge limiting beliefs, and trust that your unique path has value. When you stand firmly in your purpose, you don't just impact your own life—you empower others to do the same. Purpose is contagious; when you live in alignment with it, you become a source of inspiration, proving that fulfillment isn't found in chasing someone else's definition of success but in honoring what truly matters to you.

"At its core, purpose is rooted in intentionality—choosing to align your actions with your values and aspirations each day. It's not something you stumble upon by chance but something you cultivate through mindful choices. As you nurture it, purpose grows clearer and stronger, offering guidance through life's uncertainties. Even during times of doubt or transition, it remains an anchor, reminding you that your journey is unfolding as it should.

Reigniting your purpose isn't a one-time event; it's a continuous practice of self-awareness and realignment. It requires shedding old narratives, embracing change, and staying open to new possibilities.

The key is trusting the process, knowing that every experience whether joyful or challenging is shaping you into the person you are meant to become. When you fully embrace your purpose, you step into a life of meaning, fulfillment, and unshakable inner peace."

Why We Lose Sight of Purpose

"Purpose is never truly lost; it often gets buried beneath the weight of stress, expectations, unhealed wounds, and self-doubt. Over time, survival takes precedence over fulfillment, leading us to disconnect from what truly matters.

Consider how often we conform to external pressures—whether by silencing our dreams, playing small to avoid judgment, or deferring our passions for practicality. These compromises dim our purpose, creating an internal void. The good news is that your purpose still resides within you, waiting to be reignited.

Recognizing the factors that have distanced you from your purpose is the first step toward realignment.

One of the most common reasons we lose sight of our purpose is the overwhelming demands of daily life. Responsibilities—whether professional, familial, or societal—can consume so much of our time and energy that we forget to check in with ourselves. When each day becomes a series of obligations and expectations, self-reflection takes a backseat, and purpose feels more like a luxury than a necessity. However, purpose is not an extra; it is the foundation of a meaningful life. When neglected for too long, we may find ourselves feeling unfulfilled, disconnected, or as if something essential is missing."

Unhealed emotional wounds can create barriers between us and our true purpose. Painful past experiences—such as rejection, failure, loss, or betrayal can foster a fear of pursuing what we genuinely desire. We may unconsciously link purpose with vulnerability, remembering times when our dreams were dismissed, our efforts unrecognized, or our ambitions met with resistance. As a defense mechanism, we suppress the very things that once brought us joy and meaning. But the truth is, healing and purpose are deeply intertwined. When we allow ourselves to process and release past pain, we create the space for purpose to resurface with renewed clarity and strength.

Self-doubt is another powerful force that clouds our sense of purpose. The fear of not being "good enough" or the belief that our contributions don't matter can trap us in hesitation. We may compare ourselves to others who seem more accomplished, confident, or certain of their path, convincing ourselves that we are unqualified to pursue what truly calls us. But purpose is not about perfection or competition—it is about alignment. It's about embracing our unique strengths and understanding that our journey will unfold in its own time. When we stop waiting for the perfect moment or the perfect version of ourselves, we can begin the work of rediscovering and reigniting what has always been within us.

Society also plays a role in the erosion of purpose. From a young age, we are often conditioned to value productivity over passion, security over self-expression, and approval over authenticity. Many chase career paths, relationships, or lifestyles that appear successful from the outside but feel empty within. This dissonance occurs when we mistake external achievements for inner fulfillment. True purpose, however, is deeply personal. It is not dictated by trends, cultural norms, or other people's definitions of success. Reconnecting with purpose requires the courage to redefine fulfillment on our own terms to step away from what I's expected and toward what is true.

Ultimately, losing sight of purpose is not a sign of failure; it is a natural part of the human experience. Life's twists, turns, challenges, and transitions can pull us in different directions, sometimes far from the path we once envisioned. But just as the sun remains hidden behind the clouds on the stormiest days, our purpose is never gone—it is simply waiting to be uncovered once again. By acknowledging what has distanced us from it, we take the first step toward reclaiming it, realigning with it, and allowing it to guide us forward.

Exercise: Purpose Rediscovered

Objective: Reflect on a Moment of Deep Fulfillment to Reconnect with Your Essence

Describe a Purpose-Driven Moment: Think of a time when you felt truly aligned—engaged, confident, and impactful.

- ❖ Where were you?
- ❖ What were you doing?
- ❖ Who were you with?
- ❖ What emotions were you experiencing?

Reflection Questions:

- ❖ What aspects of this moment made you feel purposeful?
- ❖ Are those aspects present in your life today? Why or why not?
- ❖ What changes can you make to reintroduce these elements into your life?

Resetting the Table for Purpose: Decluttering for Clarity

Reigniting your purpose begins by resetting the table of your life. Imagine your life as a table filled with commitments, relationships, and aspirations. Over time, this table becomes cluttered with distractions, making it difficult to see what truly matters. What was once a carefully arranged setting—full of intention and meaning—may now be overwhelmed by obligations, expectations, and outdated beliefs that no longer serve you. Just like a cluttered table makes it hard to enjoy a meal, a cluttered life makes it difficult to connect with your purpose.

Start by asking yourself: What's taking up space that could be better used for growth or fulfillment? Perhaps it's an outdated belief, a limiting mindset, or an unfulfilling obligation. Maybe it's an attachment to an identity that no longer aligns with who you are becoming. The commitments, habits, and relationships we once accepted without question may now be preventing us from stepping fully into our purpose. By identifying and removing these "cluttered dishes," you begin the process of creating space for what truly nourishes your soul.

Decluttering for clarity is not just about letting go; it's about making conscious choices. It's about deciding what stays on your table and what needs to be removed. Some things, like old fears or doubts, may need to be discarded completely. Others, like relationships or goals, may need to be redefined or adjusted to align with your evolving sense of self. This process is not about loss—it's about refinement. By being intentional with what you allow to remain, you ensure that everything in your life contributes to your growth and purpose, rather than distracting from it.

Practical Steps for Mental and Emotional Decluttering

If resetting your table feels overwhelming, start small. Focus on one area of your life—whether it's your physical space, relationships, or mindset. Here are some actionable steps:

Assess Your Space for Alignment

Your external environment often reflects your internal state. Take a moment to look at your home, workspace, or even your digital environment. Are they cluttered with items, commitments, or reminders that no longer serve you? By decluttering your surroundings, you can create the mental clarity needed to refocus on your purpose.

Identify and Challenge Limiting Beliefs

Write down one limiting belief that drains your energy and prevents you from fully stepping into your purpose. It might sound like: "I'm not qualified enough," "I don't have time," or "What if I fail?" Once you've written it down, challenge it: Is this belief absolutely true? What new belief could better serve your growth and transformation?

Reevaluate Commitments and Relationships Ask yourself: Does this commitment or relationship align with my purpose? If not, consider how you can set boundaries, release outdated goals, or shift your focus to what truly matters. Let go of obligations that drain you and instead invest in those that bring meaning and inspiration.

Create an Action Plan for Change

Decluttering is an ongoing process, not a one-time event. Start with a small, manageable goal—such as reducing distractions, having a difficult conversation, or carving out time for self-reflection. Each step, no matter how small, builds momentum toward a life aligned with your purpose.

Journal to Reinforce Your Vision

Writing is a powerful tool for clearing mental clutter. Journaling allows you to process emotions, recognize patterns, and solidify the vision of the life you want to create. Use prompts like:

- What areas of my life no longer align with my purpose?
- What must I release to move forward? What new habits or mindsets will help me gain more clarity?

By regularly resetting the table of your life, you allow your purpose to take center stage. This process isn't about erasing the past; it's about creating the space needed for growth, transformation, and a deeper connection to what truly matters. When you clear away what no longer serves you, you make room for the opportunities, relationships, and experiences that will nourish and sustain your purpose moving forward.

Exercise: Releasing and Welcoming

Objective: Clarify what no longer serves you and what you want to welcome into your life.

Divide the Page into Two Columns:

- **Releasing:** List habits, thoughts, or commitments that drain your energy.
- **Welcoming:** List new perspectives, goals, or passions you want to cultivate.
- **Action Step:** Select one item from each column and outline a specific action to release or embrace it this week.
- **Protecting Your Purpose:** Managing Your Energy Bank. Think of your energy as a bank account—limited but replenishable. Every action, conversation, and commitment functions as either a deposit or a withdrawal. Without mindful management, you risk depletion, leaving you disconnected from your purpose.

Steps to Maintain Balanced Energy:

- Identify activities that nourish and sustain you, such as mentorship, creative pursuits, or self-reflection.
- Recognize energy-draining commitments and establish firm boundaries.

- Align your actions with your values and priorities to maintain balance and prevent burnout.

Exercise: The Energy Bank

Objective: Monitor and optimize your daily energy flow.

Identify Your Energy Deposits:

- Activities that restore and energize you
- People who inspire and uplift you
- Moments when you feel aligned with your purpose

Recognize Your Energy Withdrawals:

Tasks that leave you feeling drained or unfulfilled Unnecessary commitments that consume your time without adding value Negative or toxic interactions that sap your motivation Reflection Questions: Do you notice recurring patterns in what drains or replenishes your energy?

What small, intentional changes can you make to minimize energy drains and maximize replenishing activities?

Observing and Enhancing Your Circle: The Role of Community in Purpose

Your purpose thrives in environments that foster growth. Just as plants need the right soil, sunlight, and nourishment to flourish, your sense of purpose is shaped by the people, communities, and relationships you engage with. Every interaction either nurtures, challenges, or diminishes your purpose. The key is to discern which connections fuel your growth and which ones hold you back.

Relationships act as mirrors, reflecting both your highest potential and your insecurities. The people closest to you shape how you see yourself, how you pursue your goals, and whether you remain aligned with your values. Some relationships empower you, fostering self-discovery, resilience, and ambition. Others drain your energy, instill doubt, or divert you from what truly matters. That's why being intentional about who you surround yourself with is essential the right circle won't just support your purpose; they will remind you of it when you forget.

The Power of Positive Influence

Surrounding yourself with positive influences amplifies your purpose. These are the people who inspire you, challenge you in healthy ways, and push you to grow beyond your comfort zone. They see your potential even when you don't, reminding you of your strengths and holding you accountable to your goals. A supportive community offers more than just encouragement; it provides opportunities for collaboration, mentorship, and meaningful conversations that broaden your perspective.

Think about the individuals in your life who uplift you. Do you have people who celebrate your wins, challenge you with love, and encourage your personal and professional growth? These are the connections that strengthen your purpose. When you engage with those who are purpose-driven themselves, their energy, ambition, and mindset inspire you to keep evolving.

Recognizing and Releasing Negative Influences

Just as the right people elevate your purpose, unhealthy relationships can diminish it. Toxic friendships, unsupportive connections, and environments filled with doubt, competition, or negativity gradually erode your confidence, making you second-guess your path. If certain relationships leave you feeling drained, discouraged, or unseen, it may be time to reassess their role in your life.

Pay attention to how you feel after an interaction. Do you walk away motivated or depleted? Do they support your dreams, or do they dismiss them? Recognizing these patterns empowers you to set boundaries and safeguard your energy. Protecting yourself doesn't mean severing ties abruptly but rather redefining relationships in a way that prioritizes your well-being and growth.

Building a Purpose-Driven Community

Creating a supportive environment begins with intentionality. If you feel disconnected from those who align with your purpose, take proactive steps to seek out new spaces where like-minded individuals gather. This could mean joining a professional network, engaging in creative or spiritual communities, attending workshops, or deepening connections with those who already uplift you.

Here are ways to strengthen your circle for purpose-driven growth:

- **Seek Mentors and Role Models** – Identify individuals who embody your values and aspirations. Learn from their journeys, seek their guidance, and allow their wisdom to shape your own path.
- **Cultivate Relationships with Growth-Oriented Individuals:** Surround yourself with people committed to self-improvement and purposeful living. Their ambition and mindset will challenge and inspire you.
- **Offer Value and Support to Others:** Purpose thrives in reciprocity. As you seek support, be intentional about uplifting those around you. Helping others discover their path strengthens your own.
- **Create Safe Spaces for Vulnerability and Growth:** True purpose flourishes in environments where you can be authentic, share your fears, and receive encouragement without judgment. Invest in relationships where openness is welcomed.

Your Circle, Your Choice

At its core, evaluating and shaping your circle is about making empowered choices. You are not obligated to maintain relationships that diminish your light. Instead, you have the power to cultivate a community that aligns with your vision, fuels your passion, and affirms your worth. Your environment should reflect the future you are building, not just the past you've lived.

When you surround yourself with purpose-driven individuals, you generate momentum that keeps you inspired, motivated, and aligned with your highest self. Purpose is not a solitary pursuit—it is strengthened, tested, and illuminated through the right connections. Choose your circle wisely, and watch your purpose thrive.

As always, take a moment to reflect. Grab your journal and try one or more of the exercises below. Move at your own pace, and continue growing as you live in alignment with your purpose!

The Circle Audit

Evaluating your relationships helps you determine which ones align with your purpose. While some connections require nurturing, others may need to be distanced.

Exercise: The Circle Audit

Objective: Evaluate your relationships and their impact on your purpose.

Categorize Your Circle:

- Amplifiers (Support Your Growth)
- Neutral (No Significant Impact)
- Drainers (Diminish Your Energy and Purpose)

Reflection Questions:

- How can you spend more time with amplifiers?
- What boundaries do you need to set with drainers?
- How can you cultivate relationships that align with your purpose?

Unlocking and Harnessing Your Gifts: The Power of Purpose

Your gifts are not just talents or skills—they are the essence of who you are. They are the natural inclinations, strengths, and passions that bring you joy, energize you, and enable you to contribute meaningfully to the world. When you unlock and embrace your gifts, you do more than develop a skill set—you awaken a deeper sense of purpose. Too often, we overlook or undervalue our gifts, dismissing them as unimportant or failing to recognize their impact. But your gifts were not given to you by accident. They are part of your unique design, woven into your being to serve a purpose that only you can fulfill. When you align with your gifts, you align with something greater than yourself—a calling, a sense of meaning that extends beyond personal fulfillment and into the lives of those around you.

Harnessing your gifts means more than just recognizing them—it means actively using them, refining them, and allowing them to guide your path. Whether your gifts lie in creativity, leadership, problem-solving, compassion, or innovation, they are meant to be expressed.

Your gifts are a bridge between who you are and how you impact the world. They fuel your passions, shape your contributions, and create a ripple effect that extends far beyond what you can see. Living in alignment with your gifts leads to a sense of ease and flow—where your actions feel meaningful, your work feels fulfilling, and your life feels purpose-driven. Your gifts are not meant to remain locked away.

They are meant to be explored, nurtured, and shared. The more you step into them, the more you step into the fullest expression of yourself, allowing your purpose to unfold naturally. Now is the time to embrace what has always been within you. Unlock your gifts. Harness their power. And step fully into the purpose you were meant to fulfill.

Exercise: Defining Your Gifts

- **Objective:** Identify your strengths and explore ways to use them intentionally.

- **Create a Gift Map**: Write your name in the center and list your gifts around it.

Reflection Questions:

Which of these gifts bring you the most fulfillment?

How can you use one of these gifts more intentionally this month?

- **Action Step:** Choose one gift and write down three ways to integrate it into your life.
- **Practicing Reciprocity:** Balanced Energy Exchange
- Purpose flourishes when relationships are built on mutual exchange. Like a river, relationships need both giving and receiving to sustain growth.

Exercise: Practical Reciprocity

Objective: Create balance in giving and receiving.

Express Gratitude: List three people who have poured into you recently and find a way to thank them.

Restore Balance: Identify one relationship where energy is unbalanced and write down one action to restore reciprocity.

Through these exercises and reflections, you have taken meaningful steps toward reigniting your purpose. Each action—whether setting boundaries, redefining relationships, or aligning with your gifts—has brought you closer to your most authentic self. By clearing mental and emotional clutter, strengthening your support system, and reconnecting with what fuels you, you have laid the foundation for a life driven by intention and fulfillment. These shifts, though sometimes subtle, have the power to transform the way you see yourself and the path ahead.

But remember, your purpose is not a destination; it's an ongoing journey that will last a lifetime. It will evolve with you, deepening through each new experience, challenge, and revelation. There will be moments of doubt, detours that test your commitment, and seasons when clarity may waver—but none of these mean you've lost your way. Purpose isn't about having all the answers; it's about remaining open to the questions. The foundation you've built through these practices prepares you for continuous growth and alignment, giving you the tools to realign whenever necessary. Now, you move forward with renewed clarity, knowing that your purpose is always within you—ready to be ignited, expressed, and shared with the world. Trust that you are exactly where you need to be, and that every step you take in alignment with your truth strengthens your impact. Your purpose is not meant to remain hidden; it is meant to shine, inspire, and create a ripple effect of meaning and transformation. Step boldly into the life you are meant to live, knowing that your purpose is your greatest source of power.

Chapter 7
A State of Essence

Introduction: The Completion of a Journey

As you turn the page to this final chapter, pause for a moment to breathe and reflect on the incredible journey you've just completed. From Chapter 1 to Chapter 6, you've worked tirelessly to rediscover your radiance, redefine your relationships, and establish practices that honor your essence. The road hasn't been easy—there were moments of discomfort, challenge, and growth—but through it all, you've taken deliberate and courageous steps toward reclaiming the light within you.

Now, you stand at the threshold of something remarkable: A State of Essence. This state is not something you have to strive for. It's not a goal or destination, but the natural result of all the work you've done. It is the effortless expression of your true, authentic self, where your energy aligns fully with your purpose and your radiance flows freely into every area of your life.

The journey of reclaiming your radiance was just the beginning. In this chapter, you will take everything you've worked for and begin to live from your essence—not as an occasional experience, but as a daily reality. Here, you'll learn how to embody your true self, sustain and amplify your radiance, and share it with the world.

A State of Essence isn't about achieving perfection or living in a constant state of bliss—it's about being true to who you are, allowing your inner light to guide you through every decision, interaction, and challenge. You no longer have to force your radiance into existence; it becomes effortless. This chapter is about fully embracing your authentic self and learning to live from that place, creating a life that's aligned, balanced, and profoundly fulfilling.

1. Living from the Heart of Your Essence

At the core of A State of Essence is a deep, unshakeable connection to your inner truth. It's a state where your thoughts, feelings, actions, and energy are fully aligned with who you truly are. There's no need for external validation or approval because you understand that your worth is inherent, not dependent on the opinions or expectations of others. When you live from your essence, validation no longer comes from outside—you give it to yourself by honoring who you truly are.

Living from the heart of your essence means embracing all parts of yourself—your strengths, weaknesses, gifts, and challenges. This holistic embrace allows you to show up as your truest self in every moment. Imagine how different your life could be if you could always trust your ability to be yourself, no matter the circumstances. Living in your essence means having the courage to let go of the masks you've worn and reveal the true beauty within.

In this state, you become more attuned to your inner voice. When you're living from your essence, decisions become simpler. You feel the pull of what resonates with your truth and what doesn't. Whether it's a career choice, a relationship, or a personal goal, you begin to understand what aligns with your authentic self and learn how to say “yes” to what nourishes your soul and “no” to what drains it.

2. Living Authentically

One of the most empowering aspects of A State of Essence is living authentically. Authenticity isn't just about being "real" with others; it's about being real with yourself. This means accepting all aspects of yourself—your fears, desires, flaws, and aspirations. By doing so, you free yourself from the pressure to conform, to be someone you're not, or to live up to an image of perfection.

Living authentically involves shedding the conditioning and limiting beliefs imposed upon you by society, family, or peers. You release the fear of judgment, the need to fit in, and the desire to be liked. Instead, you become centered in your own truth, knowing that who you are, at your core, is more than enough. Living authentically is an act of self-love and radical acceptance.

Exercise: To further embrace your essence, take a few moments each day to ask yourself these questions:

- What part of myself have I been hiding or suppressing?
- What do I truly desire, free from external influence?
- What action can I take today to live more in alignment with my authentic self?

By consistently asking yourself these questions, you strengthen your connection to your essence and reinforce the power of authenticity in your life.

Sustaining Your Radiance: A Lifelong Practice

Living in A State of Essence isn't a one-time achievement—it's a lifelong practice. Just as you nourish a garden to ensure it continues to bloom, you must nourish your essence and radiance. The tools you've used throughout this journey, such as protecting your energy, observing your circle, and unlocking your gifts, are practices you can continue to implement as you move forward

Sustaining your radiance begins with ongoing self-awareness. It requires regularly checking in with yourself to ensure you're staying true to your essence and making choices that align with your highest good. Just as physical health is maintained through exercise, the practice of remaining aligned with your essence demands continual nourishment—mentally, emotionally, and spiritually.

One of the most vital aspects of sustaining your radiance is protecting your energy. Along this journey, you've learned to set boundaries, eliminate energy drains, and create nurturing environments. Now, it's time to make these practices a habit. Dedicate time each day for self-care rituals that recharge you—whether through meditation, journaling, walking in nature, or simply being still. These rituals are your way of re-centering and returning to your essence, especially during times of stress or uncertainty.

Another key element in sustaining your radiance is embracing impermanence. Life is ever-changing, and so too is your energy.

Some days, your essence flows freely and effortlessly; other days, it may feel like a struggle to stay aligned. This is normal. Embrace the ebb and flow of life, knowing your essence is always present, even when it seems distant.

3. Moving Beyond the Self: The Ripple Effect of Your Essence

As you step deeper into a State of Essence, you'll realize that your essence doesn't exist in isolation. When you live authentically and align with your true self, you naturally create a ripple effect that touches everything around you. Your energy influences the people you interact with, the spaces you inhabit, and even the opportunities that come your way. This ripple effect is powerful. By being in alignment with your essence, you begin to influence the collective energy around you, inspiring others to connect with their own radiance.

Living in your essence inspires others to do the same. People are naturally drawn to authenticity. When you embrace your full, unfiltered self, you give others permission to do the same. This leads to more genuine connections, more meaningful relationships, and a deeper sense of community.

The key here is generosity. As your radiance expands, share it freely with the world. You have gifts, wisdom, and light to offer, and by doing so, you help others see their own potential. Whether through acts of kindness, offering guidance, or simply being present, you create a space where others can also thrive in their essence.

The Power of Recognition

Recognizing the gifts in others is essential to living in a State of Essence. As you deepen your connection to your own radiance, you begin to see the radiance in others. Recognition is a powerful tool that amplifies the light in both you and those around you. When you acknowledge and celebrate the gifts in others, you create a space where everyone's radiance can flourish.

Exercise:

Identify someone in your life whose radiance has inspired you. Write them a note or tell them how their energy has impacted you. This simple act of recognition not only uplifts them but also reinforces the power of your own radiance.

4. Trusting the Flow of Life: Embracing Life's Uncertainty

Living in a State of Essence doesn't mean that life becomes predictable or free from challenges. It means that, regardless of what happens, you trust yourself and the flow of life. You trust that every experience—whether good or bad—is an opportunity for growth. You know that your essence is unshakeable and that you can handle whatever comes your way. When life throws challenges your way, your essence becomes your anchor. Instead of reacting with fear or resistance, you meet each situation with grace and adaptability. Challenges transform into opportunities to deepen your connection to your inner truth, refine your essence, and further align yourself with your purpose.

A critical part of this trust is understanding that life is constantly evolving. A State of Essence is not static; it is dynamic and ever-growing. Just as you continue to expand and evolve, so too does your radiance. Trusting the flow of life means embracing the unknown with open arms, knowing that it is all part of your journey toward greater self-realization.

5. The Interconnectedness of All Things

As you move deeper into a State of Essence, you begin to experience a profound sense of interconnectedness with everything around you. This interconnectedness is not just a conceptual idea but a lived reality. You see that everything—every person, every event, every opportunity—is connected to you in some way. Your essence is not isolated; it is part of the greater whole.

This interconnectedness fosters empathy, compassion, and understanding. You see others not as separate from you, but as reflections of your own light. True connection occurs when we recognize that we are all part of the same energy, the same essence.

Living in a State of Essence means seeing beyond the surface and recognizing the divine energy that flows through all things. Whether it's a conversation with a friend, a walk-through nature, or a moment of stillness, you feel deeply connected to everything and everyone around you. This connection enriches your experience and reinforces your understanding that your essence is not just for you—it is for the world.

6. Celebrating Your Radiance: Honoring the Journey, Embracing Your Light

"As you pause in this moment of reflection, take a deep breath and allow yourself to fully appreciate the journey you've embarked on. You have done the deep, intentional work to reconnect with your authentic self, reclaim your radiance, and step into your essence with clarity and confidence. This is no small feat—this is a profound transformation that deserves recognition and celebration.

Living from your essence is both powerful and liberating. It means you are no longer defined by external expectations, past limitations, or self-doubt. Instead, you are rooted in your truth, moving through life with purpose, authenticity, and unwavering self-awareness. This is a monumental achievement—one that has come from courageously looking inward, facing hidden pains, releasing what no longer serves you, and choosing—again and again—to align with the fullest expression of who you are."

Honoring Your Growth and Transformation

"Take a moment to reflect on how far you've come. Consider the times when you questioned yourself yet kept moving forward. Think about the barriers you've broken, the patterns you've rewritten, and the self-love you've nurtured along the way. Every step you've taken—no matter how small—has shaped the person you are today. You are living proof of what happens when intention meets action, when self-reflection leads to self-liberation.

Growth isn't just about reaching a destination—it's about becoming, evolving, and deepening your connection to your essence. This journey has shaped you, strengthened you, and illuminated parts of yourself that were once hidden. You've embraced vulnerability as a gateway to power, self-discovery as a path to freedom, and authenticity as the foundation of your existence."

Your Radiance as a Gift to the World

"Your transformation doesn't exist in isolation. By stepping fully into your radiance, you not only enrich your own life—you contribute to the collective light of the world. When one person chooses to live authentically, it creates a ripple effect, inspiring others to do the same. Your courage, growth, and commitment to your essence serve as a beacon of possibility for those still searching for their path.

Think of the times you were inspired by someone's authenticity, when another person's light encouraged you to step into your own. Now, you are that person for someone else. Your radiance invites others to embrace their truth, shed the layers of fear and conditioning, and step into the brilliance of their own being. Your existence, as it is, is a gift."

A Life Lived in Essence

"As you move forward, know that living in your essence isn't a destination—it's a way of being. It's the daily choice to honor your truth, nurture your energy, and align your actions with your values. Some days will feel effortless, while others will challenge you, but through it all, your radiance remains. Celebrate yourself—celebrate your resilience, growth, and willingness to do the work. You've arrived at a place where you're no longer chasing something outside of yourself; you're simply being, fully and beautifully. And in that being, you shine.

Your light is needed. Your essence is powerful. Your journey continues, and the world is brighter because of it."

Conclusion:

A New Beginning

As you step fully into A State of Essence, you're not just finishing a book—you're embracing a new way of being. You've done the deep, intentional work of reclaiming your radiance, protecting your energy, and aligning with your purpose. You've faced discomfort, challenged old beliefs, and created space for the person you were always meant to be. This is not the end of your journey—it's the beginning of living authentically, effortlessly, and in harmony with your true self.

Through each chapter, you've uncovered the power within you to protect, observe, unlock, and reignite—the very foundation of POUR. You've learned to set boundaries that honor your well-being, cultivate relationships that uplift and inspire, embrace your unique gifts, and reconnect with your purpose in ways that feel true and fulfilling. The work you've done is not just self-improvement; it's self-liberation. It's a declaration that you're worthy of a life that reflects your highest values, deepest passions, and truest essence.

But remember, A State of Essence isn't about perfection—it's about presence. It's about showing up for yourself every day with grace and self-compassion. There will still be challenges, moments of doubt, and times when you need to reset. But now, you have the tools, awareness, and confidence to realign whenever life calls for it. Growth isn't a destination; it's a continuous unfolding, a lifelong return to who you truly are beneath the noise of the world.

Your radiance isn't just for you—it's meant to be shared. As you continue to evolve, the energy you embody will inspire those around you. Your courage to live authentically will create ripples of change, opening the door for others to step into their own truth. You're a light, a force, a presence the world needs.

So, step forward boldly. Step forward with courage, confidence, and love. The work you've done has set you free, and now, you have the power to live in that freedom every day. Your radiance is undeniable, your essence is extraordinary, and the world is waiting for you to shine."

Made in the USA
Columbia, SC
12 July 2025

b79f0f3e-bd76-4b7c-a02f-40cf0cf5c1beR01